BY ROBERT PINSKY

POETRY

Sadness and Happiness (1975)

An Explanation of America (1979)

History of My Heart (1984)

The Want Bone (1990)

The Figured Wheel (1996)

PROSE

Landor's Poetry (1968)

The Situation of Poetry (1977)

Poetry and the World (1988)

TRANSLATIONS

The Separate Notebooks, by Czeslaw Milosz (1983)

The Inferno of Dante (1994)

THE

SOUNDS

OF

POETRY

THE

SOUNDS

OF

POETRY

A

BRIEF

GUIDE

ROBERT

PINSKY

Farrar, Straus and Giroux

New York

Farrar, Straus and Giroux
19 Union Square West, New York 10003

Copyright © 1998 by Robert Pinsky
All rights reserved
Distributed in Canada by Douglas & McIntyre Ltd.
Printed in the United States of America
Designed by Cynthia Krupat
First edition, 1998

Library of Congress Cataloging-in-Publication Data
Pinsky, Robert.
    The sounds of poetry : a brief guide / Robert Pinsky. — 1st ed.
        p.   cm.
    Includes bibliographical references and index.
    ISBN 0-374-26695-6 (alk. paper)
    1. Oral interpretation of poetry.   I. Title.
PN4151.P55   1998
808.5'4—dc21   *98-18873*

Permissions appear on page 131

To Biz

Contents

Nor is there singing school, but studying

Monuments of its own magnificence.

—WILLIAM BUTLER YEATS, *"Sailing to Byzantium"*

THE

SOUNDS

OF

POETRY

Introduction

The idea in the following pages is to help the reader hear more of what is going on in poems, and by hearing more to gain in enjoyment and understanding.

Every speaker, intuitively and accurately, courses gracefully through immensely subtle manipulations of sound. We not only indicate, for example, where the accent is in a word like "question," but also preserve that accent while adding the difference between "Was that a question?" and "Yes, that was a question."

It is almost as if we sing to one another all day.

We do not need to be taught such things: if they were taught in school, we would find them hard and make a mess of them.

In this regard, the way we use the sounds of language is like the way we use "down" and "up" with certain English verbs: I have never heard a child, however small, or anyone, however stupid, make a mistake when discriminating among such expressions as: "Can you put me up?" and its cousins—"Don't put me down," "It brings me down," "I wasn't brought up that way," "Then what it comes down to is, why bring it up?" and so forth. If we learned these distinctions by making charts and memorizing them, or by rules, we would blunder.

It is the same with what Robert Frost calls "sentence sounds."[1] Because we have learned to deal with the sound patterns organically, for practical goals, from before we can remember, without reflection or instruction or conscious analysis, we all produce the sounds, and understand them, with great efficiency and subtle nuance. Because of that skill, acquired like the ability to walk and run, we already have finely developed powers that let us appreciate the sound of even an isolated single line of poetry—even if we have very little idea of the meaning—that someone might quote with appreciation, like,

The fire that stirs about her, when she stirs

Or,

In a smart burnoose Khadour looked on, amused

Or,

Absence my presence is, strangeness my grace

Or,

Back out of all this now too much for us

Or,

Let be be finale of seem

Or,

Further in Summer than the Birds

Or,

Sorrow is my own yard[2]

The hearing-knowledge we bring to a line of poetry is a knowledge of patterns in speech we have known to hear since we were infants. If we tried to learn such knowledge by elaborate rules or through brute, systematic memorization, then just as with the distinctions involved in *putting up with me* and *putting me up*, we would not be able to use them as fluently as we do.

And yet, having learned these graceful, peculiar codes from the cradle—the vocal codes that poets have used to make works of art—we can gain a lot by studying the nature of what we learned long ago without study: learning to hear language in a more conscious way can enhance our pleasure in lines and poems. Athletes, by study or coaching, can learn to walk or run more effectively.

Study of that kind is the intention of this book: to enhance the reader's pleasure in poetry through knowledge of a few basic principles and their tremendous effects. I try to explain the principles in plain language, with a minimum of special terms, objectively, by paying close attention to particular poems and specific words. Technical language, vague impressions about the emotional effects of sounds (the supposedly exuberant or doleful *w*'s, the anxious or sensual *t*'s, etc.), elaborate systems, categories that need memorizing, little accent marks and special typographical symbols—all these, I work to avoid.

This is a brief guide: my goal is not an all-inclusive map but a brief, plain, accurate presentation of the most important points. More exhaustive approaches characterize such good books as Alfred Corn's *The Poem's Heartbeat*, Harvey Gross's *Sound and Form in Modern Poetry*, John Hollander's *Rhyme's Reason*, and James McAuley's *Versification*. In these sources the reader can find excellent accounts of terminology, detailed discussion of exceptions and anomalies, aesthetic and semantic theories, definitions and examples of received forms.

A wonderful historic account is John Thompson's *The Founding of English Meter*, from which I have learned a great deal. Thompson's book first sent me to George Gascoigne's sixteenth-century "Certayne Notes of Instruction Concerning the Making of English Verse or Ryme," the first such essay in English and still one of the best.

Often, I quote some poetry without identifying the author. (In such cases, the poet is identified in the notes at the back of the book.) The purpose is to defer interesting matters such as a given poet's reputation, themes, biography, historical context, and so forth, in order to concentrate for the moment on this book's one subject: the sounds of poetry in English.

Theory

There are no rules.

However, principles may be discerned in actual practice: for example, in the way people actually speak, or in the lines poets have written. If a good line contradicts a principle one has formulated, then the principle, by which I mean a kind of working idea, should be discarded or amended.

Art proceeds according to principles discernible in works of art. Therefore, if one is asked for a good book about traditional metrics, a good answer is: *The Collected Poems of William Butler Yeats*, or *The Complete Poems of Ben Jonson*. Two excellent books about so-called free verse are the two-volume *Collected Poems of William Carlos Williams* and *The Collected Poems of Wallace Stevens*. One of the most instructive books on short lines is *The Complete Poems of Emily Dickinson*. To learn a lot about the adaptation of ballad meter to modern poetry, an invaluable work is *Thomas Hardy: The Complete Poems*. No instruction manual can teach as much as careful attention to the sounds in even one great poem.

But a guide can be helpful. The theory of this guide is that poetry is a vocal, which is to say a bodily, art. The medium of poetry is a human body: the column of air inside the chest, shaped into signifying sounds in the larynx and the mouth. In this sense, poetry is just as physical or bodily an art as dancing.

Moreover, there is a special intimacy to poetry because, in this idea of the art, the medium is not an expert's body, as when one goes to the ballet: in poetry, the medium is the audience's body. When I say to myself a poem by Emily Dickinson or George Herbert, the artist's medium is my breath. The reader's breath and hearing embody the poet's words. This makes the art physical, intimate, vocal, and individual.

Other conceptions of poetry might include flamboyantly expressive vocal delivery, accompanied by impressive physical presence, by the poet or a performer; or the typographical, graphic appearance of the words in itself, apart from the indication of sound. Those areas are not part of this book's conception.

Ezra Pound wrote that poetry is a centaur. That is, in prose, one aims an arrow at a target. In a poem, one does the same thing, while also riding a horse. The horse I take to be the human body. Poetry calls upon both intellectual and bodily skills.

I hope to focus on the way an extraordinary system of grunts and mouth-noises evolved by the human primate has been used as the material of art. Poetry in this vocal and intellectual sense is an ancient art or technology: older than the computer, older than print, older than writing and indeed, though some may find this surprising, much older than prose. I presume that the technology of poetry, using the human body as its medium, evolved for specific uses: to hold things in memory, both within and beyond the individual life span; to achieve intensity and sensuous appeal; to express feelings and ideas rapidly and memorably. To share those feelings and ideas with companions, and also with the dead and with those to come after us.

I

ACCENT AND

DURATION

What determines the stress or accent in English words and sentences? What precisely does it mean to say, for example, that we stress the first syllable in the word "rabbit" and the second syllable in the word "omit"? What exactly does the voice do to create that audible, distinct accent? (A term that for now I will use interchangeably with "stress.")

This is a more interesting question than might appear at first. Just considering the question can, in itself, help one to hear more about the sounds of the words we speak.

For instance, the answer that stress is produced by increased loudness or volume is not completely satisfactory, as a little experimentation will suggest. Consider what a speaker does to distinguish between, say, the first word and the last word of the following sentence:

Permit me to give you a permit.

Turning the volume down or up has some relation to what our voice does, but fails to explain the delicate but quite distinct difference that virtually all speakers can indicate and virtually all listeners can detect.

I'll focus more minutely for a moment. Here is an English sound:

it

In the nature of the English language, the sound, which happens also to be a one-syllable word, is neither stressed nor unstressed, by itself. It is neither short nor long, by itself.

The sound is conventionally stressed, relative to the syllables near it, when one says "bitter" or "reiterate" or "she had wit." It is conventionally unstressed when one says "italicize" or "rabbit" or "*Pat* had it."

These examples demonstrate a useful principle: the stress on a syllable in English is not inherent in the sound, but relative. A syllable is stressed or unstressed only in relation to the syllables around it. As a corollary, accent is a matter of degree. This knowledge is useful because if accent or stress is a matter of degree, we can hear interesting rhythms even in a line where the basic structure is the simple pattern of alternating unstressed and stressed syllables. For example:

> It is not growing like a tree
> In bulk, doth make man better be.[1]

Each of these two lines is made of four pairs of syllables. Each pair of syllables is arranged so that the second one has more accent than the first: "is" sticks out just a bit more than "It" in the very light first pair; and "grow" sticks out more than "not" in the rather heavy second pair; and "like" sticks out quite a lot more than "-ing"; and "tree" definitely sticks out more than "a." In the final pair of the line ("a tree"), the difference between the unstressed first syllable and the stressed second syllable is greater than in the earlier pairs. We could analyze the second line similarly, noting that the considerable pause early in the line also varies the rhythm.

What is interesting is that within the simple system of four pairs, each pair ascending in accent from first syllable to second, the actual rhythm of the words is not singsong or repetitious, because so much varies. Unless you make the mistake of pronouncing the words in some special, chanting or "poetic" manner, you can hear both the pattern and the constant variation. The degree of accent varies and the degree of difference between the unstressed and stressed syllable also varies, from one pair to the next.

In fact, the syllable "not," unstressed within its pair, has about the same or even more stress than the syllable "is," which is stressed within its pair. Thus, the first four syllables in the line ("It is not grow-") actually ascend in degree of accent. From such observations, we can conclude that the line is not simply a thump on every other syllable: a diagram of the line would not be a series of equal hills and valleys, sawtooth fashion, but a much more varying, precise graph, with the stressed syllable in one relatively light pair sometimes on a level with, or even below, the unstressed syllable of a relatively heavy pair. Here the graph might show stairs, or four ascending points. (Something like this happens in the second line, in the first four syllables of the following phrase: "doth make man better be.")

A technical name for the pattern I have been describing as a "pair" of syllables, with the first syllable less prominent than the second, is an "iambic foot" or "iamb." The stressed syllable is determined only in relation to the other syllables within the foot. Thus, a stressed syllable within one foot may be less stressed than the unstressed syllable in another. As the imaginary graph of a line like

It is not growing like a tree

indicates, not all iambic feet are alike. In fact, no two are the same.

It has taken me many words to describe only a little of what we hear when we hear the two lines spoken and perceive, in an instant, both the abstract pattern or system (four pairs of syllables per line, the second half of each pair accented) and the actual, living rhythm of the lines. The laborious process of description, compared to the lightning apprehension, dramatizes how efficient the form is, and how sensitive the ear.

To return to the original question: what does the ear so precisely and delicately hear the voice doing?

Volume or loudness does not satisfactorily explain

what we do when we accent a syllable, because pitch—
or, most precisely, change of pitch, ordinarily higher
pitch—plays a major part in signaling the accent. Thus,
it is not merely fanciful to say that in a way we sing all
day to one another, when we speak:

"What was it? What was the question?"

"I'll tell you the question—it was, will you or won't
you permit me to have a learner's permit? Is it permis-
sible, idiot?"

"You sound so embittered."

—

The last word above, "embittered," illustrates another
important distinction. I have said that the syllable "**it**,"
or any syllable in English, is accented or unaccented only
relative to the syllables around it, not in itself. I added
that the syllable is, in itself, neither short nor long—
and this second statement is not a mere rephrasing of
the first. Long-and-short, a matter of duration, is not the
same as accent.

That fact is demonstrated by such words as "popcorn":
the first syllable is stressed. But saying the word aloud
a few times, and listening carefully, will indicate clearly
that the second syllable is longer—the sound lasts
slightly but distinctly longer. In the word "ocean," in
contrast, the first syllable is both stressed and longer.

Thus, sometimes duration reinforces accent, and
sometimes it contrasts with accent. In the word "embit-
tered," the accented second syllable is much shorter than

the rather long final syllable: duration contrasts with accent, with a certain audible effect. In the word "confounded," which has the same accent pattern as "embittered," the accented second syllable is much longer than the rather short final syllable: duration reinforces accent, with a quite different audible effect.

Duration (also called "quantity") is distinct from accent, and like accent it comes in relative degrees. Like accent, quantity is not an off-or-on-toggle. This can be demonstrated by taking the syllable,

it

and making it longer in duration by changing the vowel to a longer sound:

ought

or longer still by changing the consonant sound from the unvoiced "t," which does not use the larynx, to the voiced "d," which does use the larynx:

awed

This matter of long and short is a matter of sound, not spelling, as is demonstrated by the relatively short sound, spelled with many letters:

picked

as contrasted with the relatively longer sound

odd

The reader who cannot immediately hear the fine distinctions I am making should not panic: it is not a matter of some mysterious gift, but of habits, vocabulary and a kind of attention. It is as though I were trying to analyze the complex process of walking into the roles of the various muscles and bones in legs and feet.

The reader who wonders what difference these fine distinctions can possibly make to anyone—why care?—is invited to inspect some actual lines of poetry, with the distinctions in mind.

For example:

Now winter nights enlarge
The number of their hours,
And clouds their storms discharge
Upon the airy towers.[2]

Each line consists of three pairs of syllables (allowing the extra syllable in the rhyme "towers/hours"), and each pair of syllables falls— just as in the previous example—into the pattern of first syllable less stressed than the second.

But there is nothing monotonous or singsong, in a way nothing "regular," about the way these lines sound, if you don't pronounce them some special way that overemphasizes the less-stressed then more-stressed pattern of each pair. If you say the lines in a natural way, without thumping at the pattern, without pausing unnaturally at the ends of the lines, and without any hammy overexpressive "interpretation," you hear an attractive rhythm. I encourage the reader to say the lines aloud, letting the voice keep going, as the sentence does, with no stilted pause after the verb "enlarge" or the verb "discharge," and with no special emphasis on the accented syllables:

Now winter nights enlarge
The number of their hours,
And clouds their storms discharge
Upon the airy towers.

I think that if a reader understands that accent is relative, and that it comes in degrees, and understands, moreover, that accent is sometimes reinforced by quantity (a synonym for "duration"), and sometimes not, then the reader will better perceive the attractive, dance-like rhythm in these lines.

Here is a specific analysis to show what I mean. In the first line, the three pairs of syllables (the technical word for such a pair or unit is "foot," plural "feet") create a pleasing effect of crescendo: changes in degree of accent, changes in the difference between the unaccented and accented parts of each foot, changes in quantity, and the way the verb "enlarge" swells or reaches over the line ending toward its object "The number"—all of these elements contribute to the process of crescendo over the three feet, in three corresponding stages.

More minutely: in the first foot, the difference between the unstressed and stressed syllables is relatively slight, with the longer but unstressed syllable "Now" preceding the shorter but stressed vowel in the first syllable of "winter." The effect is a kind of acceleration from the long, unstressed syllable to the short, stressed one, with maybe some sense of tension in what might be called the "interference pattern" between quantity and accent. Then, in the second foot, the difference between the two halves is more distinct, with maybe a less strained or tense movement, because here the duration and accent are in less conflict, though the unstressed syllable of the foot (the "ter" of "winter") is pretty long in quantity. And in the final, third foot, which consists of the word "enlarge," the difference between the two halves is quite distinct: duration and accent both emphasize the second syllable of the word.

This little movement is from quick and tense toward increasingly slow and luxuriant.

It is worth pointing out that while the line moves from some tension to the fullness and resolution of its last foot, the running-over grammar from "enlarge" to "The number" represents not resolution or completion but an extending reach. And these sentences describe only some of the energies that course through the lines and make them feel alive:

Now winter nights enlarge
The number of their hours,
And clouds their storms discharge
Upon the airy towers.

No writer would think this way—muttering to one-
self about short and long, stressed and unstressed—any
more than a jazz musician would think that a series of
dotted eighths and sixteenth notes might make a nice
contrast to the triplets of a preceding bar, or a boxer
would ponder whether to fake a right cross to make
more room for the jab. The expert makes the moves
without needing to think about them. But the more we
notice and study, the more we can get from actual per-
formance. And analysis of a fluid performance into its
parts can lead to understanding, and perhaps eventually
to the expert's level of insight and the expert's kind of
joy.

What I have said about the opening lines of "Now
winter nights enlarge," with their three iambic feet, ap-
plies equally to so-called free-verse poems that are not
written in iambic feet. For instance:

One must have a mind of winter
To regard the frost and the boughs
Of the pine-trees crusted with snow,

And have been cold a long time
To behold the junipers shagged with ice,
The spruces rough in the distant glitter

Of the January sun, and not to think
Of any misery in the sound of the wind

Here too, variations in degree of accent, variations in the difference between an unaccented syllable and an accented syllable, and a varying play between accent and duration all have a part in creating the rhythm.

More specifically, the relatively short vowel sound found in the word "it," somewhat lengthened in the word "winter," involves a contrast between pitch and accent. That is, the stressed syllable in the word is shorter than the unstressed syllable. The line

One must have a mind of winter

generates a lot of movement in its short space partly through other variations between pitch and quantity: the stressed first syllable followed by three increasingly more rapid, relatively lighter syllables before the slowing, full syllable "mind," which is both stressed and pretty clearly the longest syllable in the line. Then the shorter but stressed first syllable of "winter" speeds things up again, in a different way—so that the line moves from slow, to rapid, to slower, to another kind of speed.

(In the first line of Campion's "Now Winter Nights

Enlarge," the same word is part of a quite different movement: the stressed syllable of the word, in Campion's line, is the first of three progressively longer stressed syllables.)

Free verse like that of "The Snow Man" moves partly by avoiding the unstressed-stressed pattern of iambic feet: thus, the cluster of three rapid syllables "must have a" functions to keep the rhythm from slipping into iambs. On the other hand, the poem does not fall into mere prose, either; achieving such intensity of rhythm is sometimes a matter of putting longer or stressed syllables next to one another, as in the third line:

Of the pine-trees crusted with snow,

where the three syllables "pine-trees crust" serve an intensity that is not iambic and that is not prose.

That intensity has a lot to do with quick, distinct variations in pace, an alert movement from fast to slow and back, in varying degrees, as in the line

The spruces rough in the distant glitter,

where after the iambic beginning of the line a light, rapid series of syllables ("in the distant glitter"), quick as a fish, breaks up the pattern. The reverse movement, from fast to slow, light to heavy, characterizes an earlier line,

And have been cold a long time

But it may be time to stop concentrating on syllables and separate lines, before such concentration gets monotonous, and proceed to larger units. The passage I have quoted is part of a poem that happens to consist of a single sentence. Here is the entire poem (by Wallace Stevens):

The Snow Man

One must have a mind of winter
To regard the frost and the boughs
Of the pine-trees crusted with snow,

And have been cold a long time
To behold the junipers shagged with ice,
The spruces rough in the distant glitter

Of the January sun, and not to think
Of any misery in the sound of the wind,
In the sound of a few leaves,

Which is the sound of the land
Full of the same wind
That is blowing in the same bare place

For the listener, who listens in the snow,
And, nothing himself, beholds
Nothing that is not there and the nothing that is.

I invite the reader to say this poem aloud, without undue pauses at the ends of lines, trying to listen for variations in accent and duration, respecting such variations and their effect on pace, rather than relying on expressive interpretation.

But accent and duration, and the variation in each, and their varying relation to one another, are only part of a poem's bodily, vocal presence. The larger flow of syntax inside and across lines, as in the single sentence of "The Snow Man," also deserves attention.

II

SYNTAX AND

LINE

What is a line of poetry?

To put the question more precisely, what vocal reality underlies the typographical convention of stopping at the right margin and returning to the left margin? (*Versus* in Latin, from which the word "verse" derives, signifies the ploughman at the end of a furrow turning about to begin again, so that "verse" and "reverse" are closely related.)

I will deal with the question by looking at some poems, beginning with an example that seems particularly conscious of its own lines. The author, Ben Jonson (1572–1637), conveys in his title that a lady to whom he has given his picture (no small gift, in the days before photography) subsequently left that gift in Scotland (a wild, remote place, to a Londoner of the time—no small distance to leave any valued object behind). In response, Jonson writes:

My Picture Left in Scotland

I now think, Love is rather deaf than blind,
        For else it could not be
            That she
Whom I adore so much should so slight me,
        And cast my love behind.
I'm sure my language to her was as sweet,
        And every close did meet
    In sentence of as subtle feet
        As hath the youngest he
That sits in shadow of Apollo's tree.

Oh, but my conscious fears,
        That fly my thoughts between,
        Tell me that she hath seen
    My hundred of gray hairs,
    Told seven and forty years,
    Read so much waste, as she cannot embrace
    My mountain belly and my rocky face;
    And all these through her eyes have stopped her
        ears.[1]

The evidence of this poem indicates that whatever else
a line may be, it is not necessarily a unit that is the
same length throughout a given poem. On the contrary,
Jonson seems to delight in varying the line length. One
line consists of a single iambic foot: "That she." Quite a
few lines consist of three iambic feet: "And every close

did meet" or "That fly my thoughts between." And there is one line that consists of four iambic feet (only one such line, a fact no reader is likely to notice unless, as right now, counting for purposes of study): "In sentence of as subtle feet." And there are some longer lines, of five feet, including those with which Jonson begins and ends his poem.

Therefore, judging by "My Picture Left in Scotland," a line is not necessarily a unit of equal length throughout a poem. On the other hand, the lines do unmistakably have a certain rhythm in common, an artful coherence: part of the pleasure the poem gives is hearing that rhythm while the sentence courses over it, or through it, or along with it, or whatever spatial language you like to describe the way we hear the sentence-sound—the voice saying what Jonson chose to say—continuing through the iambic lines of varying length.

I find an appealing show-off quality to the lines in this particular poem. Cupid, the classical god of love, is traditionally blind; Jonson chides the one who has not loved him enough by accusing her of paying more attention to the surfaces her eyes see than to the movement of the words he offers. So he makes the sentences perform like the body of a great dancer, as the syntax —the words in their arrangement, and the dynamic energy the arrangement creates—sometimes pauses at a line ending, and sometimes streaks or leaps or strains across it. There is a pronounced pause after the first line, then the syntax runs over from the second line to the third, and even more from the very short third to the fourth, with more of a pause after the fourth line, and a full stop after the fifth:

> I now think, Love is rather deaf than blind,
>> For else it could not be
>>> That she
> Whom I adore so much should so slight me,
>> And cast my love behind.

The run-over lines and pauses, the varying line lengths, the varying way the unit of syntax (that is, the grammatical phrases) coincides with the unit of rhythm (that is, the lines) or does not coincide—all of these create an expressive, flamboyant whole. The poem speeds up and slows down many different ways in the course of these five lines. Though the lines are all made of iambic feet, the variation in pace and emphasis is great—greater than could be easily attained in a comparable thirty-one words of prose.

I invite the reader to say the words of Jonson's poem aloud, taking care not to pause in a stilted way at the ends of the lines, when the grammar runs over. Try to pause only as the grammar might pause, if necessary exaggerating the effect a little to hear what the author has done. The rhymes (for instance, "For else it could not be/That she/Whom I adore so much should so slight me") are not lost when the voice carries pretty rapidly through them: on the contrary, they sound better than when the voice stops mechanically at each one. I think that if one tries reading the poem with an even pause after each line, the movement goes dead.

One way I think of the related movement at such moments in a poem is that the syntax is trying to speed up the line, and the line is trying to slow down the syntax. The relation between the two elements, the resulting pull or dance, is pleasing and expressive.

There is an analogy to be made here: just as in the previous chapter the examples indicated the infinite range of expressive possibilities as accent and duration sometimes coincide to reinforce one another, sometimes differ, in ever-varying degrees—so the example of "My Picture Left in Scotland" suggests an infinite range of expressive possibilities as the unit of syntax and the line sometimes coincide to reinforce each other, sometimes differ, in ever-varying degrees.

There are as many different kinds of line ending as there are ways one word can follow another: sometimes the line is rather violently trying to slow down the sentence, while the sentence is trying to speed up the line, as in this extreme run-over of the syntax in Hart Crane's ecstatic, mystical poem "The Dance":

> I learned to catch the trout's moon whisper; I
> Drifted how many hours I never knew

And sometimes the line ending reinforces the syntactical divisions, calling attention to the thrust and arrest of a

sentence, as in the opening subtleties of Elizabeth Bish-
op's "At the Fishhouses":

> Although it is a cold evening,
> down by one of the fishhouses
> an old man sits netting,
> his net, in the gloaming almost invisible,
> a dark purple-brown,
> and his shuttle worn and polished.

Just as no two iambic feet are alike, so no two gram-
matical joinings between words are alike; every foot is
a little different and every line ending slices into the
sentence a little differently.

From the discussion so far follows one of the most
important principles of this book: the line and the syn-
tactical unit are not necessarily the same. Much unsatis-
fying reading and much inferior writing proceeds from
not getting this idea right.

Before testing this principle against some more poems,
there is a matter of terminology and description that is
raised by the second half of Ben Jonson's "My Picture
Left in Scotland." This terminology will be discussed
again, more fully, in the next chapter; but here I will
anticipate that discussion, with a point I will return to
in more detail. Here is the second part of Jonson's poem:

> Oh, but my conscious fears,
>   That fly my thoughts between,

> Tell me that she hath seen
> My hundred of gray hairs,
> Told seven and forty years,
> Read so much waste, as she cannot embrace
> My mountain belly and my rocky face;
> And all these through her eyes have stopped her
> ears.

Although I have described this poem as consisting of iambic feet—that is, pairs of syllables in which the second syllable sticks out more in sound—the first and third lines of this passage begin with pairs of syllables that invert that order. In the pairs "Oh, but" and "Tell me," it is the first syllable, not the second, that has more "acoustic prominence" (to use the technical term for "sticks out more in sound").

Beginning a line with an inverted foot is, statistically, extremely common. The inverted or reversed order appears to be an effective way to launch the line (which is one reason I discuss it here). This initial inversion characterizes many famous quotations:

Now is the winter of our discontent

Jove in the clouds had his inhuman birth

Further in Summer than the Birds

When to the sessions of sweet, silent thought

That's my last Duchess painted on the wall

Much have I traveled in the realms of gold

Something there is that doesn't love a wall

The inverted foot, when substituted in the first position in the line, as at the beginning of the second half of Jonson's "My Picture Left in Scotland" ("Oh, but my conscious fears"), is common, and I do not hear it as much of a variation: certainly less significant a variation than the changes in degree of accent, the changing relation of accent and duration, and the changing relation of line to syntax.

Statistically less common, and a more prominent variation to my ear, is the inverted foot in the second position, as in these examples:

My heart aches, and a drowsy numbness pains

What vain art can reply

The soft voice of the nesting dove

Now no joy but lacks salt

Or in the third position:

For precious friends, hid in death's dateless night

With eager thought warbling his Doric lay

I step inside, letting the door thud shut

And more rarely (in a line long enough) the fourth position:

The beat's too swift. The notes shift in the dark

By the dark webs, her nape caught in his bill[2]

For purposes of the present discussion of lines, it is enough to think of the inverted foot as a frequent variation on the iamb, especially common at the beginnings of lines. (The technical term for an inverted foot is "trochee" or "trochaic foot," with the "ch" pronounced like "k.")

Besides sometimes being inverted, the iambic foot also sometimes has its first, unstressed part divided into two, as in the three-foot line

Told seven and forty years,

where the second syllable of the word "seven" joins the word "and" to serve together as the first, unstressed part of the second foot. The effect—bouncing two quick syllables, often elided together, into the place of one—is a rapid, even galloping rhythm. It occurs in the third foot, following the pause, in this line:

Dust as we are, the immortal spirit grows[3]

This rhythmical figure, with the unstressed half of the foot divided into two, as in "the expense," is called an "anapest" or "anapestic foot." With these two variants in mind—the inverted or trochaic foot and the anapestic foot that begins with two rapid light parts in place of one—the line of iambic feet can be understood and distinguished from the free-verse line.

Now let me continue the discussion of line and syntax, amplifying the idea that the rhythmical unit (the line) does not always coincide with the syntactical unit (the grammatical phrase). Here is another poem to read aloud:

To Earthward

Love at the lips was touch
As sweet as I could bear;
And once that seemed too much;
I lived on air

That crossed me from sweet things
The flow of—was it musk
From hidden grapevine springs
Down hill at dusk?

I had the swirl and ache
From sprays of honeysuckle
That when they're gathered shake
Dew on the knuckle.

I craved strong sweets, but those
Seemed strong when I was young;
The petal of the rose
It was that stung.

Now no joy but lacks salt
That is not dashed with pain
And weariness and fault;
I crave the stain

Of tears, the aftermark
Of almost too much love,
The sweet of bitter bark
And burning clove.

When stiff and sore and scarred
I take away my hand
From leaning on it hard
In grass and sand,

The hurt is not enough.
I long for weight and strength
To feel the earth as rough
To all my length.[4]

This poem is pretty clearly composed in vocal lines: that
is, you can hear them, and you would detect their pres-
ence without a printed version of the poem, just by
hearing it. As before, I advise the reader to read the
sentences, not treating the end of every line as an au-
tomatic pause. I suggest that you experiment with a sin-
gle sentence, such as

I had the swirl and ache
From sprays of honeysuckle
That when they're gathered shake
Dew on the knuckle.

Reading the sentence aloud two different ways—first, with a natural continuation of the syntax after "ache" and "honeysuckle" and "shake"; then a second time, pausing after each line—demonstrates, to my ear, that continuing rather than pausing is more attractive. It sounds better, and far from being lost the rhymes, too, sound better. To put this idea another way, reading each line differently according to the differences in syntax conveys more information: you get the information of the line as well as the information of the syntax. Ideally, you are hearing as much difference as possible, and also hearing the underlying pattern of the lines.

And if all lines were alike, then why would anyone write in lines?

The poem "To Earthward" illustrates how writing in lines can establish great variation in pace, from slow to fast. This fluid change of speed, accelerating and decelerating expressively, emerges partly from varying ways the actual words are related to a symmetrical pattern. The poem is organized into eight symmetrical units. I say "symmetrical" because each unit consists of four lines, with the first three made of three pairs (or feet) and the fourth made of two feet.

But this pattern is not treated in a monotonous manner, as we can hear.

For example, the passage about the honeysuckle, with its long words and run-over lines, dances forward rather quickly while staying within the pattern of first three lines of three feet followed by a fourth line of two feet; compare its rhythm with a later passage that also stays within the pattern, but to a much different effect.

Longer words tend to move faster than one-syllable words, and sentences whose parts keep going across the line move faster than sentences that make more of a stop at the ends of lines:

I had the swirl and ache
From sprays of honeysuckle
That when they're gathered shake
Dew on the knuckle.

For such objective causes—word length, the relation of syntax to line, and we can add even, distinct iambic feet as compared to more rapid, varying degrees of difference and accent—that passage moves more quickly, as I hear it, than this one:

When stiff and sore and scarred
I take away my hand
From leaning on it hard
In grass and sand.

Such differences are subtle, not ponderous or gross: yet they are distinct. They are not impressionistic feelings, but part of what the sounds in English do.

I have put off mentioning the little extra syllable at the end of "honeysuckle" and "knuckle." Traditionally called, for some reason, "feminine rhyme," this effect (like the extra, "galloping" syllable referred to above, which begins the phrase "the immortal spirit grows") makes for a quicker movement.

The relation of syntax to line can express very fine shades of meaning in the voice. Sometimes the effect is like the extra signals we can give in conversation, with a change in our voice, or with a facial expression or hand gesture. There is something like a gesture of the voice in the way the sentence leaps from the first four-line unit to the next, at the beginning of the poem, where it runs over on the word "air":

Love at the lips was touch
As sweet as I could bear;
And once that seemed too much;
I lived on air

That crossed me from sweet things
The flow of—was it musk
From hidden grapevine springs
Down hill at dusk?

And of course, there is a different kind of leaping in the run-over from "musk" to "From hidden grapevine springs." And I hear still another kind of grammatical reaching toward the phrase "From hidden grapevine springs," launched by the dash after "The flow of—"; the syntactical energy is like a physical act of meaning. When we say the poem aloud, it *is* a physical act of meaning.

I have used a slightly corny vocabulary, words like "dancing" and "leaping," to describe the effect when syntax does not coincide with the rhythmical unit of the line, but goes on past the line. That vocabulary echoes the technical word for what I have been calling a "run-over" or a "run-over line": enjambment, based on the French word for leg. In enjambment, or a run-over line, the syntax throws its leg over the hedge or low wall of the line.

Here is another example of the principle:

To a Poor Old Woman

   munching a plum on
   the street a paper bag
   of them in her hand

   They taste good to her
   They taste good

to her. They taste
good to her

You can see it by
the way she gives herself
to the one half
sucked out in her hand

Comforted
a solace of ripe plums
seeming to fill the air
They taste good to her[5]

Although this poem is not composed in iambic lines but
in so-called free verse, the element of symmetry is clear:
each unit, if we count the title as part of the first unit,
has four lines. (The technical term for these symmetrical
units, separated by white space, is "stanza," the Italian
word for "room.")

Even more than "To Earthward," this poem treats its
four-line stanzas as syntactical wholes; "To Earthward"
sometimes runs over from stanza to stanza; "To a Poor
Old Woman" never does. In fact, the second stanza in
this poem is given over to repetitions of a single, five-
word sentence.

The poet (William Carlos Williams) gives us a phrase,
"They taste good to her," first as a whole and then an-
alyzed differently by the line. The notion of a vocal ges-
ture applies here, too. As in "To Earthward," the varying

intersection of syntax and line, sometimes in agreement and sometimes in an interference pattern, is precisely expressive. That is, the tension between syntactical unit and rhythmical unit—the line trying to slow the sentence down, the sentence trying to speed up the line—gives a somewhat different emphasis to the phrase each time.

First we get the five-word phrase in its whole prosaic form, end-stopped. Then the analytic effect of the line cutting across the sentence emphasizes first the predicate adjective "good," then the verb "taste" with the pronoun "they" as its subject (the word "plums" does not appear until two stanzas later), and finally at the end of the stanza the isolated phrase "good to her." When the repeated sentence comes back in the last line, fitted entire into a line again, it is informed by our memory of the separate emphases of the second stanza.

These rather solemn explanations neglect the feeling, and the poem's material. There are some plums, and a woman, and they taste good to her; also, there is a poet eager to direct the reader toward the complex web underlying an experience so simple a child could articulate it: they taste good to her; you can see it.

In "To Earthward," the yearning, stretched-forward quality of the vocal gesture persists through the youthful, exquisite sensibility stung by rose petals and the later, older sensibility "stained" by tears; you could say that the relation of syntax and line in that poem conveys that quality. In the context of the explicit meanings of the words, the pattern of sounds has moral force: it, too, means something.

The repetitions in "To a Poor Old Woman" also have that kind of moral force, made explicit by the phrase "you can see it." The poem dramatizes the taking in of a supposedly ordinary experience, and the playful, almost hectoring repetitions are like an effective sermon in praise of simplicity. The quality of the goodness and the subjective experience of tasting are visible to the observer. The energy lurking inside the adjective "good" or inside the syntax coursing through five monosyllables indicates the energy of the senses, a force so powerful that you can see it in another person. The varying recurrence becomes a way of saying how simple such seeing is, and how difficult. The heightened perception of the stripped, plain phrase, made memorable in its rhythm and meaning, parallels the heightened perception of the visual scene.

This resource, the angling of syntax into line and stanza at interesting tilts, rather than in an end-stopped, four-square manner, is supremely important. The variations of enjambment; the beautiful end-stop after Frost's "The hurt is not enough" or after Williams's "Comforted"; the play between the symmetries of stop and of return; the lines on one side and the twists of each sentence on the other—these are an important part of the pleasure in poetry.

An aside: In their relation of speech-syntax to line, and in their relation of vocal alertness to sensory alertness, "To Earthward" and "To a Poor Old Woman" have much in common. Yet their respective authors, Frost and Williams, are conventionally viewed as extremely different, even opposite, kinds of American poet.

To conclude this chapter, here is a little exercise: a poem arranged in two different ways, typographically. Assume for the moment that the sound is the same either way—that is, assume that the sound of "My Picture Left in Scotland" or "To Earthward" or "To a Poor Old Woman" would be there even if we typed the poems up as blocks of prose: it would just be much harder for the reader to detect the sound. In this theory, the poem is something one hears aloud, and the poem in print is a notation designed to make what one hears as clearly apprehensible as possible.

With that assumption, which of the following two arrangements gives the most useful and helpful information about the poem they represent? Which is preferable?

VERSION A
Pictures from Breughel, X
(Children's Games)

This is a schoolyard
crowded with children
of all ages
near a village
on a small stream meandering by

where some boys are swimming bare-ass
or climbing a tree in leaf

everything is motion

elder women are looking after
the small fry
a play wedding
a christening

nearby one leans hollering
into an empty hogshead

VERSION B
*Pictures from Breughel, X
(Children's Games)*

This is a schoolyard
crowded
with children

of all ages near a village
on a small stream
meandering by

where some boys
are swimming
bare-ass

or climbing a tree in leaf
everything
is motion

elder women are looking
after the small
fry

a play wedding a
christening
nearby one leans

hollering
into
an empty hogshead

A reader might have sensible reasons for preferring Version A: it avoids one-word lines, it does not cross the flow of the syntax with such violent enjambments as "small / fry" or "a / christening", it attains a certain clarity and ease by presenting units of thought such as "everything is motion" within single lines. For corresponding reasons, Version B will seem choppy, perverse and unnatural to some readers.

And yet, Version A is something I produced in as little time as it takes to type it; I tried to arrange the lines the way I think most beginning poetry students would tend to do it. Version B, on the other hand, is the poem as composed by William Carlos Williams. I don't believe that one should take the superiority of B as a matter of authority, however; if it can't be demonstrated why the author's version is better, the question should be open.

Such demonstration requires thinking about what the poem means. By asking what, precisely, it is about, one can begin to form a judgment about how it should sound, and therefore about what arrangement in lines best brings out those vocal rhythms for the reader.

The poem describes a painting by Peter Breughel, a painting that apparently has many separate focuses of energy, and a lot of movement. To speak precisely, since it is a painting, I should say the illusion of a lot of movement. As though aware of that fine distinction, or the way movement in the static medium of paint is an illusion, Williams seems deliberately to violate a great creative writing dictum: he uses the verb "is" almost exclusively. This "is" a schoolyard, the boys "are" swimming or climbing, and the elders "are" looking after the small fry.

Young writers are exhorted to make their verbs specific, and to avoid the passivity of the verb "to be." Here, that verb and the many participles (the meandering, climbing, swimming, looking, hollering) seem to call attention to the paradox of motion in something static.

Even the generalization, "everything is motion," depends on the verb "to be." The participles are emphasized by other "-ing" words that resemble them: "wedding," "christening," and perhaps even "everything." Every stanza after the first one contains at least one word that ends in "-ing," again emphasizing the ideas of activity and, if not stasis, a kind of eternal present for each activity: this painted stream keeps meandering forever, and so too the painted children keep on swimming and climbing and hollering and the painted elders keep on looking. (This distribution of words in "-ing" symmetrically over symmetrical stanzas is lost in Version A.)

There is one exception to the participials and the verb "to be," and that is in the poem's one active, inflected verb, delayed until almost the very end:

a play wedding a
christening
nearby one leans

hollering
into
an empty hogshead.

The active verb "leans" is effectively placed here, I think, stretching in the enjambment across the space that precedes the last stanza. As with Frost's run-over from "I lived on air" in his first stanza to "That crossed me from sweet things" in the second, the effect of pouring across suits the meaning, and therefore what the voice does in continuing rather than stopping, quite well.

It is also worth noting that the verb "leans" deserves

its emphasis in another way: it denotes both an activity and a state. That is, in a sentence like "he leans down to pick it up," the word indicates an active process. But in a sentence like "the tower leans, as it was noted to do shortly after it was built," the word indicates a stable condition. Thus, in spilling over to "hollering" in the last stanza, the word continues the double or perhaps even paradoxical nature of Williams's description.

Some readers will find in the final action of hollering to create an echo a reflection of the poem's theme: imitating in paint or words what has occurred in nature. The painting echoes certain activities, and the poem echoes those activities and the painting. This notion gives a further appropriateness to the enjambment

    everything
    is motion

because there is a kind of philosophical or metaphysical weight that the tension of enjambment emphasizes. Because the sentences are tilted in the frame of symmetrical stanzas and lines, they have more motion and also more weight.

I created Version A by treating each line as a grammatical unit: prepositional clauses, modifiers, all the natural pauses, allowing myself a slight enjambment, out of boredom I think, on the word "after." If this were what writing in lines meant—that the lines simply follow the units of syntax, with no tension or tilting—the question I have mentioned before would arise: why write in lines? It is the potential to vary—a potential which affects even an end-stopped line, when the writing is good—that gives the art its point.

I think one can learn a lot by typing a poem up as a block of prose and then, working from that block, trying to arrange it in lines that you think bring out the rhythms in the most effective way possible. How would one distribute the different kinds of emphasis? Where should the emphasis of enjambment go? On which words should the emphasis of beginning a line go? On which words should the emphasis of ending a line go? Which faster and slower passages are most crucial? Where should the emphasis of the end-stop go?

Then, after completing what seems the most successful typographical arrangement, and listening to what it seems to indicate about the rhythms of the sentences, one can compare the new version to the original, the lines as composed by the author. It doesn't seem impossible to me that occasionally the new arrangement, designed for the exercise, might have some virtue the actual poem lacked. Either way one learns something.

Less formally, a mental process like such an exercise —being aware of how a thing is done, and appreciating more by noticing more—is the goal of this book. That goal is the justification for the terminology which has been generated so far, and which will be elaborated in the next chapter.

III

TECHNICAL TERMS AND

VOCAL REALITIES

The material in this chapter is not as important as that in the first two chapters; there, in discussing first accent and duration, then syntax and line, I have tried to demonstrate some of the ways in which the sounds of a poem work. The way each of those four elements varies, both in itself and in its varying relation to the others, seems profoundly interesting to me.

In this chapter, I will discuss the choice of terms to describe such elements.

No aspect of a poem is more singular, more unique, than its rhythm. I have tried to show that no two syllables, no two iambic feet, no two degrees of accent or duration, are quite alike. Therefore, it is clear that each line, each poem, has a rhythm different from all others. If this is true about iambic poems, then presumably it is even more true of poems in free verse. This principle has been illustrated by comparing various units, each of three iambic feet, and all with quite different rhythms:

When stiff and sore and scarred

The number of their hours

And all these through her eyes[1]

The wide range of difference possible within a basic pattern is even more dramatic with a longer line, as in these examples, all with five feet:

And with old woes new wail my dear time's waste

In having its undeviable say

The house was quiet and the world was calm

—and looked and looked our infant sight away

From that smoothe tongue whose music hell canst move[2]

The vocal reality, in other words, is individual and distinct in ways too subtle for any terminology or system to describe completely. At most, only the simple outline or structure (as in "three feet in each line" or "an inverted foot at the beginning") can be described.

Many writers on the subject make this point by distinguishing between the terms "rhythm" and "meter": rhythm is the sound of an actual line, while meter is the abstract pattern behind the rhythm, roughly analogous to the way 4/4 time in music underlies the actual dotted eighths and sixteenths and so forth. Rhythm is the reality, in this distinction, and meter (a term derived from the Greek word for "measure") is the ruler-like symmetry. A ruler or rectangular grid can give useful information about an irregular or complex shape; meter can be thought of as doing something similar in relation to the irregular, complex sounds of speech. Though hardly essential for appreciating the sounds of poems, this distinction is sensible, and I encourage the reader who agrees to use it.

A refinement or corollary to the rhythm-meter distinction, for some writers, is to make a parallel distinction between stress and accent: assigning stress, with rhythm, to the approximate emphases of speech; and assigning accent, with meter, to the more artificial, regular divisions of metrical feet. Again, the reader who likes the distinction should use it. Certainly it helps distinguish what can be described or measured from what cannot.

What I conclude from the impossibility of describing the countless differences in rhythm among lines and poems and phrases is that the terminology should be simple, informative, and minimal. It should be as universal as possible, by which I mean that it should cover the maximum number of cases with the minimum number of terms. It should try to describe the meter—the synonym "measure" was once common—and not the rhythm.

Here is a practical demonstration of that point. One could devise many different descriptive approaches, all equally sensible, to describe some of the poems previously discussed. For instance, I have said that this passage

Love at the lips was touch
As sweet as I could bear;
And once that seemed too much;
I lived on air

can be described as three lines containing three pairs of syllables and a fourth line containing two pairs. Suggesting that a pair of syllables that ascend in accent is an iamb, or iambic foot, I asserted that such a pair or foot is the basic unit in "To Earthward." I fudged in an exception by saying that quite often the first foot in a line is reversed or inverted, as in the first two words here ("Love at").

What reason is there not to divide each line differently, for instance by describing the first line,

Love at the lips was touch,

as two feet: one *thunketta* ("Love at the") followed by a *thunk-pa-thunk* ("lips was touch")? Though I have invented somewhat silly-sounding terms, they make sense: they describe something all can hear.

But still other descriptive terms for the same line— the same vocal reality—would also make sense. For instance, I could also describe the line

Love at the lips was touch

as an initial monosyllable ("Love") followed by an anapest ("at the lips") and an iamb ("was touch").

Or (to try the reader's patience just a little more) the

same line could be described as two feet: one that could be graphed visually as a U-shaped unit ("Love at the lips") followed by one that could be graphed as a J-shaped unit ("was touch").

Similarly, the line I have described as three iambic feet,

As sweet as I could bear,

can be rationally described as one *kathunka* ("As sweet as") followed by a *thunk-pa-thunk* ("I could bear").

What is wrong with these terms? Nothing—in the sense that, though arbitrary, they do register something that is there in the sound of the words. Each set of terms does give a roughly accurate description of what one hears. But such terms fail to concede their abstract, arbitrary nature: that is, they fail to distinguish the abstract pattern from the reality (meter from rhythm, if you like); the enterprise of such nomenclature implies that one can describe a rhythm, which is impossible.

And the terms I have invented to make this point are needlessly complicated. If I try to describe too much, proliferating extra terms to register, for instance, the similarity of the two strong syllables "too much" or the integrity of the ("U-shaped") phrase "Love at the lips," my imaginary vocabulary of thunkettas and so forth obscures the principle of similarity—iambic feet, four-line stanzas, the last line one foot shorter than the first three in each stanza—that not only unifies "To Earthward" but also connects "To Earthward" with so many other works in English. Such works include the plays of Shakespeare (written mainly in lines of five iambic feet), and writing by Frost's approximate contemporaries Wallace Stevens and T. S. Eliot.

The "thunketta" approach—trying to identify each turn of rhythm—is not simple enough, and it neglects the principle that the rhythm varies in relation to the meter.

Such a method of description lacks universality, not only because the iambic foot does a superior job of clarifying the relation of "As sweet as I could bear" to the rest of "To Earthward" and the rest of poetry in English, but because all sorts of other possible descriptions make as much sense.

What we hear can be described in many different ways. The question is: which is the most useful system? I conclude that the most information about the unique, varying vocal reality is given by the simplest, most modest set of terms: something minimal and therefore approaching the universal, like the lines on a ruler or the grid of rectangles an artist might use to copy an image.

When I hear the four words "that seemed too much," my noticing that they comprise two iambic feet helps me hear more about their sound. It helps me notice that the stressed and unstressed halves of each foot are very close to each other, with the change in pitch distinguishing them. To call them "four heavies" or "a long-long followed by another long-long" tells less, in my opinion, through undertaking to describe more than is possible.

I have tried to make this point by using the opening lines of "To Earthward" because the lines are by now familiar to the reader, and because three-foot lines are relatively easy to hear. But the point—that there are many alternate ways to attempt describing the rhythm, but a simple understanding of the meter tells more—is even stronger with the five-foot line. Here are four such lines:

When to the sessions of sweet, silent thought
I summon up remembrance of things past,
I sigh the lack of many a thing I sought,
And with old woes new wail my dear time's waste.[3]

These lines sound good to me. Thinking about their elegance of sound, I describe the passage to myself something like this: each line has five iambic feet. The first line has the familiar trochaic, or inverted, foot at the beginning ("When to"). In the last line, some of the iambs are made of two syllables so close in prominence ("old woes," "new wail") that they are practically equal, though I like hearing the slight change of pitch throbbing through them. I hear a similarly slow-but-onward, throbbing movement when four syllables in a row ascend in accent, in the first line: "-sions of sweet, si"—the pattern where the stressed syllable of one foot has less stress than the unaccented syllable that begins the next foot. In fact, this ascending pattern is echoed by the movement in that fourth line, where the differences between unstressed and stressed halves of the iambs almost, but I think don't quite, dissolve. I also notice, in the third line, after three quite distinct iambic feet ("I sigh the lack of ma-") the lightly bouncing anapest, with the unstressed half divided into two, in the fourth foot, and the clear iamb in the fifth: "-ny a thing I sought."

Even when I am uncertain, this simple pattern of five iambs per line helps me hear the varying energy that pleases me in the passage. Even when I am not sure if the difference between stressed and unstressed halves of "old woes new wail" is there, or that I can hear it, even when I am not sure whether to let the pattern dictate an iambic pronunciation of "And with" or to consider it an inverted foot, the simplicity and universality of the terms help me notice the sounds.

And this is the beginning of a sonnet by William Shakespeare. The pattern of five-foot lines rhymed this way, with this kind of syntax, relates the poem to other lines by Philip Sidney and Thomas Wyatt, which Shakespeare might have read, and relates the poem also to other lines by John Keats and Wallace Stevens and Sylvia Plath, writers in five-foot lines who, I know, have read these lines.

If I describe the first line to myself as a *thunketta* ("When to the"), another *thunketta* ("sessions of"), a *strong-strong* ("sweet, si-"), and an iamb ("-lent thought"), making four feet, I am telling about something real, and telling it accurately, but I am losing the simplicity, the clarity, and the widespread application of plainer terms, by which I mean the iamb and its variations. Because the longer line of the sonnet invites even more subpatterns than the shorter one of "To Earthward," more rhythmical relations and possibilities exist. Trying to describe that rhythm rather than the meter, I attempt to perceive more, but in fact I perceive less. The simple unit, the iambic foot, helps me perceive the general aesthetic principle, like a time signature or the grooves on a dial, that guides me through the infinite, actual variety.

That is how the iamb or iambic foot has been so basic. Because the stressed syllable is determined only in relation to the other syllable or syllables in the foot, one can hear the rising and falling and turning of the line as a whole, yet also hear a principle of order.

I don't know why the iamb has been basic, and I doubt that anyone can say.[4] Certainly it is not true to say that the language "is iambic." It is worth noting that English does not have the inflected grammatical endings that characterize some other languages, and so instead uses monosyllabic words to make certain distinctions: *of, his, their, from, this,* for example. Many English words are trochaic: *people, hungry, country, cattle, farming, worker, color, catcher, winter.* A lot of iambic lines are made of trochaic words and monosyllables:

The seagull's wings shall dip and pivot him

The sweet of bitter bark

Now winter nights enlarge

In sentence of as subtle feet

When to the sessions of sweet, silent thought

This is so much the case that when Elizabeth Bishop writes a five-foot line with three iambic words in it, the effect is strange, catchy in its difference, like a samba or reggae beat:

In a smart burnoose Khadour looked on, amused.

Such interesting effects can just barely be described. Yet they may be more notable—more of a variation— than, say, the trochee or inverted foot at the beginning of the line, as in Hart Crane's

Vaulting the sea, the prairie's dreaming sod.

The trochees in both the first and the third foot in the line that begins the same poem,

How many dawns, chill from his rippling rest,

have an effect to my ear of a kind of double beginning. (Or, on second thought, should the first foot be considered an iamb?)

The third kind of foot I have mentioned, the anapest, where the first, unstressed part of the foot is divided into two, tends to speed up the line—putting two syllables into the space where one might have been. The anapest is frequently very light, the added syllable eliding or melting into the others, as in this Shakespeare line, with two quick, barely-audible anapests:

And moan the expense of many a vanished sight.

In fact, the original (pirated) printing of Shakespeare's sonnets treated the first anapest typographically as an elision:

And mone th'expence of many a vannisht sight.

The anapest in English tends toward a distinct difference between the two light, more or less elided unstressed syllables and the stressed one; the difference does not seem to vary as fluidly as it can with iambs. The effect of heavier unaccented syllables hustled along, and of many anapests jouncing by one after another, is highly conducive to comedy:

When you're lying awake with a dismal headache,
    and repose is taboo'd by anxiety,
I conceive you may use any language you choose to
    indulge in, without impropriety.[5]

With the iambic foot and these two variations on it —trochaic or inverted, and anapestic or divided—the reader can apprehend the basic structure of a great body of traditional poetry in English. And by hearing that poetry, the ear for free verse, for variations of many sorts, can be sharpened.

The purpose of the terms is to apprehend as much as possible of the vocal reality that one hears.

A few other terms, of occasional usefulness: one is "sprung rhythm." Sometimes an unstressed syllable is omitted, jamming two stressed syllables together; thus, Fulke Greville writes, about arising in the middle of the night to pursue a forbidden love affair:

> Up I start believing well
> To see if Cynthia were awake;
> Wonders I saw, who can tell?
> And thus unto myself I spake.[6]

The second and fourth lines are straightforward four-foot, essentially iambic lines. The first line omits the first syllable, and the remarkable third line omits the unstressed syllable before "who," creating a double stress "saw, who" in the middle of his line; that is, Greville did not write the more conventional lines,

> So up I start believing well
> To see if Cynthia were awake;
> Wonders I saw, that who can tell?
> And thus unto myself I spake.

This small difference, emphasizing the accents, makes the lines that much more various and, in the context of the narrative, that much more sexy—and, perhaps, less complacent and more off-balance.

Sprung rhythm refers generally to the jamming in of stressed syllables. The spectacular generator of the term is Gerard Manley Hopkins; many of his greatest lines demonstrate the border between iambic and free verse. The lines are so strong that it hardly matters which term we use:

> My cries heave, herds long, huddle in a main, a chief-
> woe, world-sorrow; on an age-old anvil wince and sing—
> Then lull, then leave off. Fury had shrieked 'No lingering! Let me be fell: force I must be brief.'

The reader ambitious to write free verse could profit from studying these formal, rhymed lines.

The most conventional place for the omitted syllable is at the beginning of the line, creating the double stress between the last syllable in one line and the first in the next. Ben Jonson, in "His Excuse for Loving," manages to write fluid sentences, with varying pauses, right across that strong, emphasized line ending:

> Let it not your wonder move,
> Less your laughter, that I love.
> Though I now write fifty years,
> I have had, and have my Peeres;
> Poets, though divine, are men:

Some have loved as old again.
And it is not always face,
Clothes, or Fortune gives the grace;
Or the feature, or the youth:
But the Language, and the Truth,
With the Ardor, and the Passion,
Gives the Lover weight, and fashion.
If you then will read the Storie,
First, prepare you to be sorry
That you never knew till now,
Either whom to love, or how:
But be glad, as soon with me,
When you know, that this is she,
Of whose Beautie it was sung,
She shall make the old man young,
Keepe the middle age at stay,
And let nothing high decay,
Till she be the reason why,
All the world for love may die.

It is interesting to note how much more rhythmical interest and emotional urgency this has than if Jonson had not omitted the syllables, and written a rhythm like:

O Let it not your wonder move,
And less your laughter, that I love.
For though I now write fifty years,
I still have had, and have my Peeres.

To me, this chatty and rhythmically dead revision demonstrates how great a difference these small matters make. When the omitted syllable occurs consistently at the beginning of the line, the lines are called "catalectic" or "beheaded."

Terms like "iamb," "trochee," and "anapest" come to us from the quantitative meters of Greek and Latin— meters based not on accent, but on duration; in those languages, syllables are long and short, not relatively but absolutely. Among the many classical terms that have been used to describe English sounds is "spondaic" (the term for a Greek or Latin foot of two long syllables). Though I have said that I hear the iambic movement in pitch right through the long, distinctly accented syllables of a line like

And with old woes new wail my dear time's waste,

it makes sense to call the rhythm "spondaic" at those moments. (Personally, I have listened so hard to English for so long, in these ways, and in particular to poetry, that I never hear an actual, perfect "spondee"; there is always at least a slight difference between the two syllables to my ear, so I prefer the adjectival form, "spondaic.")

Besides the monosyllabic foot and the spondaic movement, writers sometimes refer to a "pyrrhic foot," to describe the very light iamb followed by a heavy (or "spondaic") one, as in the third and fourth feet of a line I have discussed,

When to the sessions of sweet, silent thought

There is nothing wrong with having a term to refer to this figure; the main thing, as I hear it, is to perceive the slight step up in pitch from "-sions" to "of" and from "sweet" to "si-," because that rise in pitch over four syllables is a pleasing movement, one that contrasts with the spondaic feeling of the second pair in the group.

Students sometimes encounter the classical term "dactyl," which in Greek or Latin verse means a long syllable followed by two short ones. The term seems unnecessary to me; though it describes something we sometimes hear, as in this line of Campion's,

What if a day, or a month, or a year

It makes a kind of sense to say that this is three "dactyls" ("What if a," "day or a" and "month or a") followed by a monosyllable. But the line can be adequately described without adding this additional term—see the remarks above about clarity, simplicity, and universality—as the initial trochee ("What if"), an iamb ("a day"), and two light anapests ("or a month" and "or a year").

Turning from feet to lines, it remains to note that there is a traditional, technical language for the kinds of line I have been calling "two-foot," "three-foot," "four-foot," and "five-foot." Borrowing again from the classical system, custom names the lines like this: the line of two feet (like the fourth lines in the stanzas of "To Earthward") is called "dimeter"; the line of three feet is called "trimeter" (the predominant line in "To Earthward" and "Now Winter Nights Enlarge"); the line of four feet is called "tetrameter" (the line of "Let It Not Your Wonder Move"); the line of five feet (the line of Shakespeare's plays and sonnets, of Milton's "Paradise Lost" and Keats's "To Autumn," of Stevens's "Sunday Morning," of Frost's narrative poems, and also buried in Allen Ginsberg's "Howl" and William Faulkner's prose) is called "pentameter"; the line of six feet (rather rare) is called "hexameter."

Here are some quick additional examples for some of these lines. Trimeter, as in the examples of "Now Winter Nights Enlarge" and "To Earthward," quoted previously, is often a rather song-like, sensual measure. Examples involving dance come to mind, though the dance may be not entirely happy, as in Theodore Roethke's "My Papa's Waltz":

> The whiskey on your breath
> Could make a small boy dizzy;
> But I hung on like death:
> Such waltzing was not easy.

The measure is made dirge-like in Thomas Nashe's "Litany in Time of Plague":

> Rich men, trust not in wealth,
> Gold cannot buy you health;
> Physic himself must fade;

All things to end are made;
The plague full swift goes by

The "sensuous" or "dancing" quality may have to do simply with how frequently the line ending (and also the end-rhyme, if there is any) occurs in such a short measure. The effect is similar in some kinds of free-verse line that seem related to the trimeter (three-foot) line, as in this passage from Wallace Stevens's "Thirteen Ways of Looking at a Blackbird":

At the sight of blackbirds
Flying in a green light,
Even the bawds of euphony
Would cry out sharply.

As a present to the reader, here is a whole poem in trimeter lines, by Thomas Hardy:

The Self-unseeing

Here is the ancient floor,
Footworn and hollow and thin,
Here was the former door
Where the dead feet walked in.

She sat here in her chair,
Smiling into the fire;

He who played stood there,
Bowing it higher and higher.

Childlike, I danced in a dream;
Blessings emblazoned that day;
Everything glowed with a gleam;
Yet we were looking away!

———

The tetrameter (four-foot) line is maybe more often
used for a song-like or comic effect than the pentameter
(five foot). And the tetrameter may be harder to sustain
over quite a long poem, partly because it divides evenly
in the middle, and tends to fall into a symmetrical cen-
tral pause, as in the line "This is the cow, with crumpled
horn." T. S. Eliot lets the tendency of tetrameter to fall
into equal halves, divided by a central pause, create a
grotesque effect in the first stanza of "Sweeney Among
the Nightingales"; in the fourth line of the stanza, there's
a kind of relief or release from that pattern:

Apeneck Sweeney spreads his knees
Letting his arms hang down to laugh,
The zebra stripes along his jaw
Swelling to maculate giraffe.

Keeping the pause (technical name: "caesura") from fall-
ing monotonously in the middle is a challenge in te-
trameter. When it falls near the end or the beginning

of the line, the emotional effect can be remarkable. A good example of this effect of the pause early or late in the line is in Ben Jonson's "Excuse for Loving," quoted in full above; in these three lines, the pauses seem to me to contribute considerably to the emotion:

First, prepare you to be sorry
That you never knew till now,
Either whom to love, or how:

A free-verse counterpart to the tetrameter (four-foot) line, and also of this off-center pause, appears in Sylvia Plath's poem "Sleep in the Mojave Desert." In each of the first three lines below, there is a pause near the midpoint. Then, in the fourth line, the run-over from the words "the only," coming after the pause quite late in the line, breaks the symmetry, with an effect that I hear as increasing the urgency or restlessness. The lines from that point may become less static or closed-in:

Hot grains, simply. It is dry, dry.
And the air dangerous. Noonday acts queerly
On the mind's eye, erecting a line
Of poplars in the middle distance, the only
Object beside the mad, straight road
One can remember men and objects by.

Description can only gesture toward effects like this, which are made of so many elements. (For instance, in these lines by Plath, the rhyme of "dry" with "eye" emphasizes the heavy pause midway in the third line; and the rhyme on "by," at the end of the passage, modifies the effect further—returning as to a musical theme, but changing the theme, too.)

—

I have described the pentameter line, based on a pattern of five iambic feet, as the line of Shakespeare's plays, of Milton's *Paradise Lost*, Keats's "To Autumn," and Stevens's "Sunday Morning"; it has been described as the equivalent of 4/4 time in music or of the rectangular canvas in painting. I will look at this pentameter line in detail in the chapter entitled "Blank Verse and Free Verse."

For now, here are some one-line examples from the works I name in the previous paragraph:

To-morrow, and to-morrow, and to-morrow
    (*Macbeth*, V, v, 19)

The dark unbottom'd infinite Abyss
    (*Paradise Lost*, Book II, line 405)

Among the river sallows, borne aloft
    ("To Autumn")

And pick the strings of our insipid lutes!
    ("Sunday Morning")

I have also noted that lines and clumps of such pentameters show up in the free verse of Allen Ginsberg, and at eloquent, high moments in the prose of writers like William Faulkner and Herman Melville. Here are some lines from "Howl," rearranged typographically to reveal the iambic pentameters (the second line a little rough):

Alchemy of the use of the ellipse
The catalog the meter & the vibrating plane,
Who dreamt and made incarnate gaps in Time
And space through images juxtaposed, and trapped

Or, again with an anapest here and there, even the opening lines reveal the pentameter throb:

I saw the best minds of my generation
Destroyed by madness, starving hysterical naked,
Dragging themselves through the negro streets at
    dawn

The poem contains many such passages, as well as striking single pentameters buried in the free-verse context:

Who lost their loveboys to the three old shrews

Moloch whose mind is pure machinery!

Who barreled down the highways of the past

And "Howl" 's wonderful closing words also make a pentameter, with the trochee in its conventional first position:

Door of my cottage in the Western night

That line follows a rhythmic pattern close to this pentameter of Wordsworth's in the Tintern Abbey "Lines":

Sent up in silence, from among the trees!

Or this one by Milton in "Lycidas" (a poem Ginsberg knew by heart):

So sinks the day star in the Ocean bed

Here is a passage from Faulkner's *Absalom, Absalom!* The pentameter dissolves a bit in the middle of the passage, but recovers with a last line that, like the first, would fit into a passage by Shakespeare:

It was no madman who bargained and cajoled
Hard manual labor out of men like Jones;
It was no madman who kept clear of the sheets
And hoods and night-galloping horses with which
[Men who were once his acquaintances
Even if not his friends discharged]
The canker suppuration of defeat.

The two lines in brackets waver from the iambic pentameter a little, but the second of them ("Even if not his friends discharged") is a perfect tetrameter, with the initial foot inverted. Another wonderful moment when a pentameter occurs in prose is the peroration of W. E. B. DuBois's great essay, "Of the Training of Black Men": the first sentence of the concluding paragraph is:

I sit with Shakespeare and he winces not.

—

Alternating lines of four feet (tetrameter) and three feet (trimeter) comprise the stanza often used for ballads and hymns. The ballad stanza or a version of it often appears in poems by Emily Dickinson:

Further in Summer than the Birds
Pathetic from the Grass
A minor Nation celebrates
Its unobtrusive Mass.

And by Thomas Hardy:

The tangled bine-stems scored the sky
Like strings of broken lyres,
And all mankind that haunted nigh
Had sought their household fires.

The ballad or hymn stanza is related to the old "Poulter's measure" of alternating lines of six and seven feet (thirteen, the poultry-seller's dozen, allowing for the odd broken egg, hence "Poulter's"). Because the lines are divided by a central caesura, the effect is units of three, three, four, and three feet. Here are the first four lines of Fulke Greville's elegy for Philip Sidney:

Silence augmenteth grief, writing increaseth rage,
Staled are my thoughts, which loved and lost the
wonder of our age;
Yet quickened now with fire, though dead with frost
ere now,
Enraged I write I know not what; dead, quick, I
know not how.

If these lines were divided in half (after "grief" in the first line, after "lost" in the second, "fire" in the third, and "what" in the fourth), their resemblance would be clear to the similar stanza (three feet, then three again, then four, then once again three) in Dickinson:

The Heart asks Pleasure—first—
And then—Excuse from Pain—
And then—those little Anodynes
That deaden suffering—

As a free-verse equivalent or relative of the ballad stanza, some of Robert Creeley's poems in four-line stanzas sometimes echo the movement between four and three, while avoiding the iambic pattern, as in the beginning of his poem "The Faces":

The faces with anticipated youth
look out from the current
identifications, judge or salesman,
the neighbor, the man who killed.

Finally, a suitable transition to the next chapter will be to conclude by quoting from a kind of hyper-ballad, Edwin Arlington Robinson's "Eros Turannos" ("Love the King" or "Love the Tyrant"). Here the movement between four-foot and three-foot lines is extended into a stanza of eight lines, including a spectacular triple rhyme. Here are two of the poem's six stanzas:

She fears him, and will always ask
    What fated her to choose him;
She meets in his engaging mask
    All reasons to refuse him;
But what she meets and what she fears
Are less than are the downward years
Drawn slowly to the foamless weirs
    Of age, were she to lose him.

Between a blurred sagacity
    That once had power to sound him,
And Love, that will not let him be
    The Judas that she found him,
Her pride assuages her almost,
As if it were alone the cost.

He sees that he will not be lost,
    And waits and looks around him.

These rhymes, which can be appreciated best if the reader knows how to let the voice continue through and past them, carried on by the energy of the syntax, exemplify the material of the next chapter.

IV /

LIKE AND

UNLIKE SOUNDS

In different ways, and in varying degree, the sounds of words are similar and different.

This simple fact, almost embarrassingly obvious to state, provides the basis for a tremendous part of poetry's power.

The line from *Macbeth* which I have quoted earlier represents one extreme of likeness:

To-morrow and to-morrow, and to-morrow

That is, repetition can be thought of as the ultimate in like sounds. So rhyme, however we define it, is a matter of unlikeness as well as likeness: "to-morrow" rhymes with "sorrow" because of how the two words are like and unlike. "To-morrow" does not rhyme with "to-morrow" because they are exactly alike; it does not rhyme with "sagacity" because they are too unlike.

Here is an example of like and unlike sounds in an actual poem. The poem provides a good example because it is short (only four lines long) and rich in sounds that chime variously:

The dry soul rages. The unfeeling feel
With the dry vehemence of the unreal.
So I, in the Idea of your arms, unwon,
Am as the real in the unreal undone.[1]

The end-rhymes (*feel* with *-real* and *-won* with *-done* at the ends of the lines) make up only part of the poem's complex web of likeness and difference in sound—an audible web so attractive to me that I feel willing to trust the meaning, even while I can't quite get it, because the sounds have so much conviction and appeal.

When I do get the meaning—the imagined embrace of the desired one, which is unreal, confounds and distracts the frustrated lover who feels real absence and an unreal fantasy, dry and vehement—the compacted, fiendishly chiming nature of the sounds seems to enact that action of "raging." The emotion, the sexual horniness, produces an artifact of extravagant control.

By the audible web of sound I mean, for example, the recurrences in "the unfeeling feel" and "I, in the Idea." Both of these examples involve repetition of the same sound in a different word: in the case of "unfeeling feel," a repeated sound with the same meaning made opposite, and in the case of "I, in the Idea," a different meaning. The triad of "unwon" and "unreal, undone" involves the rhyme between the prefix "un-" and both "won" and "done."

When you consider also the rhyme between "Dry" (another repeated word) and both "I" and the first syllable of "Idea," as well as the vowel sound repeated in "real" and "Idea," the most striking aspect of the poem becomes the way it avoids jamming up, overclotted with too many like sounds. In this sense, the sounds of "soul rages," "vehemence," and "your arms" become important because they don't much recur: in a way these sounds, keeping the richness from being overdone, are the most important ones in the poem.

This example indicates that likeness and difference of sound are matters of degree. Rhyme, however one defines that term, is a matter of degree, and not necessarily an either/or toggle.

Just as the varying relation of pitch and duration, in their changing degrees, can be expressive, and just as the varying relation of line and syntax can be expressive, the varying kinds and degrees of likeness of sound can be expressive.

"The dry soul rages" demonstrates that principle in an end rhymed poem. Here are some lines from a poem that is not end-rhymed, demonstrating the same principle, I think. The poem (by Robert Frost) is in "blank verse"—that is, pentameter (five-foot) lines with no regular end rhyme; but rhyme, or something like rhyme, surely plays a great part in the poem's effect:

An Old Man's Winter Night

All out-of-doors looked darkly in at him
Through the thin frost, almost in separate stars,

That gathers on the pane in empty rooms.
What kept his eyes from giving back the gaze
Was the lamp tilted near them in his hand.
What kept him from remembering what it was
That brought him to that creaking room was age.
He stood with barrels round him—at a loss.

There is a complicated embroidery here. One thread involves like consonant sounds such as those at the end of "doors" and of "stars" and perhaps of "gathers"; or the related consonant sounds (the "s" sound called a "sibilant") at the end of "eyes" and of "gaze" and of "was," and perhaps at the end of "loss," too. But crossing that consonant-thread is another vowel-thread involving the long "a" sound in "pane" and "gaze" and "age."

Thus, in the line

What kept his eyes from giving back the gaze

the reader may hear "his" and "eyes" and "gaze" rhyming with one another and also with "was" two lines later. But the reader may also hear a likeness between the final word "gaze" and the word "pane" at a caesura (within-the-line pause) above it and the word "age" at the end of a line below it. "Hear" is a more or less figurative term here: that is, the reader doesn't necessarily think about the sounds I have compared to embroidery threads, or register them consciously. But the effect is felt, just the same: the poem almost sings in end-rhyme about this solitude, but mutes the singing quality instead: more like humming to oneself, maybe.

And all of this happens in an "unrhymed" poem.

As always, description lags, in its cumbersome way, far behind what it gestures toward. Much is always left-out, even as the sentences of description pile up. It would be interesting, for example, to think about the likeness and difference of syntax as it stretches and folds across the two units, of two lines each, which both begin with the words "What kept": the two units are parallel, but not perfectly parallel, in ways that contain and echo and contrast with the play of like and unlike sounds.

Here is a sentence from farther along in the poem, three lines that illustrate how close to the audible effect of end-rhyme a supposedly unrhymed poem can come. Listen to the terminal "t" sound (called a "dental" sound, as is that of "d") as it falls sometimes at the ends of lines, at other times after the caesura or pause within the line, at still others at no particular pause.

A light he was to no one but himself
Where now he sat, concerned with he knew what,
A quiet light, and then not even that.

To say the sentence aloud, hearing the delicate, fluctuating echo on *light, sat, what, light, that* is among other pleasures to hear the way there are pentameters within pentameters. That is, because the passage is made out of units of three and two feet, there is a kind of buried pentameter line that would read,

To no one but himself where now he sat,

if the poem were written a little differently, and another one that would read,

Concerned with he knew what, a quiet light

The terminal "t" sound marks off these possibilities with an effect of great penetration.

The poem at such points seems to tremble between blank verse and full end-rhyme, as though the old man's night is partly a matter for narration, partly for something more lyrical. The poem's conclusion continues that double quality:

And slept. The log that shifted with a jolt
Once in the stove, disturbed him, and he shifted,
And eased his heavy breathing, but still slept.
One aged man—one man—can't keep a house,
A farm, a countryside, or if he can,
It's thus he does it of a winter night.

In the last three lines, the rhyme between "one aged man" at the beginning of a line and "or if he can" at the end of another line is separated by the kind of "buried" pentameter line I've referred to—

Can't keep a house, a farm, a countryside—

And one effect of this musical, shifting, echoing quality is to intensify the widening of what "keep" means, so that the man "keeps" something as metaphysical as "a countryside." This philosophical sweep is not loud or heavy partly because, I think, the pattern of sounds provides something like a leavening counterpoint. And the repetition of the word "man," itself, reminds us that metaphysical or not, the story is also actual, present.

A free-verse poem that I have quoted at the end of Chapter I, Wallace Stevens's "The Snow Man," provides a good example of like sound in lines that are neither iambic nor end-rhymed:

The Snow Man

One must have a mind of winter
To regard the frost and the boughs
Of the pine-trees crusted with snow,

And have been cold a long time
To behold the junipers shagged with ice,
The spruces rough in the distant glitter

Of the January sun, and not to think
Of any misery in the sound of the wind,
In the sound of a few leaves,

Which is the sound of the land
Full of the same wind
That is blowing in the same bare place

For the listener, who listens in the snow,
And, nothing himself, beholds
Nothing that is not there and the nothing that is.

In the first two three-line stanzas, the similarity of "winter" and "glitter" accompanies the similarity of "mind" and the first syllable of "winter." In going from "mind" to "winter," the "i" is shorter in the second word, and the dental sound changes from "d" to "t," but the consonant clusters of "nd" and "nt" (both described technically as a "nasal" sound followed by a "dental") are reinforced by the stress that falls on them and by the many repetitions that are on the way—beginning with the sound of "pine-trees," which echoes the vowel of "mind" and the consonants of "winter."

The recurrence of the nasal-dental cluster becomes quite rich and prominent in this passage:

not to think
Of any misery in the sound of the wind,
In the sound of a few leaves,

Which is the sound of the land
Full of the same wind
That is blowing in the same bare place

For the listener, who listens in the snow,
And, nothing himself, beholds
Nothing that is not there and the nothing that is.

The repeated words "sound," "land," and "wind" make
the audible presence of like sounds so intense that their
relative absence becomes an important part of the fi
nal four lines. (I say "relative" absence because the word
"And," with its distinct pauses before and after, echoes
the rhyme-sound distinctly—a bravura touch to put so
much musical and syntactical force on so bland a word.)
Because "beholds" and "snow" and "nothing" and "is"
are quite dissimilar from mind/sound/land/wind, they
have an emphasis similar to the emphasis I tried to point
out in "The dry soul rages"; sometimes, the like sounds
serve to dramatize and heighten the unlike sounds

In a way parallel to how an enjambment is a place
where the syntax might stop, but pushes forward instead,
the shift away from a consonant sound may mark a
moment when things might chime, but depart instead.
Here, the relative absence of a consonant sound, and
its one recurrence on "and"—like the enjambment on
"beholds"—emphasizes and tempers the change from
one kind of severity to another: from the brilliant, bleak
landscape to the differently severe process of "behold-
ing."

So far, I have spoken of only one kind of likeness:
degree of rhyme. But "The Snow Man" contains a few

examples of another kind of likeness or unlikeness, such as the phrases

> January sun

and

> distant glitter

and

> junipers shagged,

all phrases in which I hear a kind of delicious contrast between the Latin and the Germanic roots, a little like that between crunchy and soft. Though the sounds are physically similar—"distant" and "glitter" with the same vowels, "January" and "sun" sharing a consonant —"distant" and "January" and "juniper" are from a subtly more abstract or scientific-sounding area of the English lexicon, while "sun" and "glitter" and "shagged" and "crusted" are from a more immediate-sounding or concrete-sounding part of the language. While the phrases involve sounds that are similar physically, the sounds of the words, in this more figurative or emotional sense of "sound," are in contrast.

This is an effect Stevens seems to like especially, and even more striking examples in his work come to mind, like the phrase in "Sunday Morning,"

> inarticulate pang,

or in these lines, from the same poem:

Nor visionary south, nor cloudy palm
Remote on heaven's hill, that has endured
As April's green endures; or will endure
Like her remembrance of awakened birds,
Or her desire for June and evening, tipped
By the consummation of the swallow's wings.

"Tipped" is from a Germanic root, akin to the Old High German word *zipf*; "consummation" is from the Latin. So, too, for each of the two-word phrases I have quoted: "January" is Latin and "sun" is Germanic; "distant" is Latin and "glitter" is Germanic; in the next phrase, it is the adjective, "shagged," that is Germanic and the noun, "juniper," that is Latin.

I think that Stevens, in his particularly characteristic way of making these Latin-Germanic pairs, may be recording his love for the poems of Keats, more than any single poet. (Phrases in Keats such as "maturing sun," "unravished bride," "dull opiate," "strenuous tongue" flood to mind.)

This expressive contrast is not limited to adjective-noun pairs. To say that "green endures" or to speak of "remembrance" of "birds" is to make the same contrast as in "visionary south." It is a contrast that calls up the history of the English language and the people who have spoken it, often invading, enslaving, raping, and torturing one another, or converting one another to new religions, or marrying one another, and changing the language in the process. The freshness or contrast suggested sometimes by yoking words with different roots calls on such history.

This contrast of roots seems to me validly a matter of sound: I think that the speaker or reader who does not know a Latin root from a Germanic root hears the difference. This is part of why a police officer afraid of being tricked by lawyers may try to hide in Latin roots:

> Simultaneously with the individual being apprehended, he indicated prior information he had obtained concerning that locality.

This way of saying "At the same time as we caught the guy, he said he knew about the place before" takes a largely intuitive, as it were ear-guided, direction. Our plain, short, rude words for bodily functions and substances and parts are Germanic: the longer, more clinical words are Latin. You don't need to know this to hear that the difference between "shit" and "excrement" is parallel to the one between "fucking" and "sexual intercourse." We *hear* the difference, without necessarily thinking about it. (The fact that we hear it is demonstrated by the phrase I have quoted, "inarticulate pang": the clearly Latinate adjective contrasts with the monosyllable "pang" in the way I have described, but to my knowledge the root of "pang" is unknown. It *sounds* Germanic.)

So, when Elizabeth Bishop writes toward the end of "At the Fishhouses," about the very cold water:

If you should dip your hand in,
your wrist would ache immediately,
your bones would begin to ache and your hand
    would burn
as if the water were a transmutation of fire

I think we hear some Germanic plainness in "your wrist would ache" contrasted with some Latinate definition in "immediately" (a word that means "without any intervening medium"—nothing coming between). And that contrast anticipates the contrast between the Germanic *bones, ache, hand, burn, water, fire*—those substantial realities —and the Latinate *transmutation*: a process that changes the substantial. The Latinate word is part of the way Bishop's poem surges upward from immediate experience to something more reflective or mysterious.

I don't mean to suggest that this combining and contrasting of roots is a conscious process for the writer, any more than it is for the reader. When Thomas Jefferson wrote of "life, liberty and the pursuit of happiness," I doubt that he was thinking of the primal, physical effect of Germanic "life," the Roman, legalistic force of Latin "liberty," the courtly, equestrian connotations of Norman French "pursuit," and the return to Germanic roots with "hap." It sounded right to him, as it sounds right to us.

Similarly, Frank O'Hara is not thinking about such matters when he writes, in "Steps":

> the apartment was vacated by a gay couple
> who moved to the country for fun
> they moved a day too soon
> even the stabbings are helping the population
>   explosion
> though in the wrong country

Part of the comic effect has to do with the way quasi-legal or ponderously journalistic terms from the Latin ("vacated," "population explosion") contrast in sound with "moved to the country for fun" and "stabbings." The contrast in roots is not necessarily for the sensuous effects of Keats and Stevens.

When Allen Ginsberg writes in "Kaddish" of "Money! Money! shrieking mad celestial money of illusion," he evokes speed and intensity of mind by the speed of motion among kinds of root. His phrases in "Howl" like "contemplating jazz" or "ultimate cunt" rely on this same rhetorical turn.

When the word with a Latin or French root rhymes with the Germanic root, we hear that, too. Thomas Hardy's "The Darkling Thrush" demonstrates his ear for this kind of expressive contrast. The poem's first stanza is:

I leant upon a coppice gate

   When Frost was specter-gray,

And Winter's dregs made desolate

   The weakening eye of day.

The tangled bine-stems scored the sky

   Like strings of broken lyres,

   And all mankind that haunted nigh

Had sought their household fires.

"Leant," "desolate," "specter," and "dregs" all share a vowel sound. "Day" and "gray" and "gate" share another—in fact, the end-rhyme of "day" and "gray," two monosyllables from the same area of the language, is potentially dull. The passage is about a spiritual dullness, and one way it resists banality is by means of certain distinctive words: unlike "gray" and "day," "coppice" and "bine-stems" and "scored" (with its brilliant evocation of both a musical score and incised scratch marks) have a lot of character.

But if the "gray/day" rhyme is a little flat, the rhymes of "desolate" with "gate" and "lyres" with "fires" gain a lot of energy because the roots differ: "desolate" from Latin "desolans" and "gate" nearly as concrete and Germanic as a noun can be. "Lyres" comes through French from the Greek, and "fires" is not only Germanic but basic, even more basic than "gate": it might be one of the first words one would learn, and it is rhymed with a classical symbol of art, poetry, and music.

Other terms for the kind of word or root I have been calling Germanic might be Anglo-Saxon or Old English. These terms call attention to yet another part of the complex matrix in "The Darkling Thrush." The alternating lines of four and three feet, and the alternating end-rhymes, recall the formal closeness of this poem to hymns and ballads. A sophisticated work, dated "December 31, 1900"—the exact turn of the century—Hardy's poem harks back to the English ballad, to folk poetry and communal singing, while it is also a literary work, well aware of predecessors like Keats's "Ode to a Nightingale." The play between modern and old, literary and folk elements, runs through the very sounds. Here is the second stanza:

> The land's sharp features seemed to be
>   The Century's corpse outleant,
> His crypt the cloudy canopy,
>   The wind his death-lament.
> The ancient pulse of germ and birth
>   Was shrunken hard and dry,
> And every spirit upon earth
>   Seemed fervorless as I.

The Germanic or Old English root "outleant" rhymes with the Latin or Romance root "lament." The hard, earthy, and northern monosyllables of the "pulse of germ and birth/Was shrunken hard and dry" are like one color, with the more southern and perhaps more learned-sounding "spirit" and "fervorless" as another one.

Given such intricate patterns of sound, in great measure intuitively heard and intuitively perceived, the pattern of end rhyme is like a grid or baseline on which a poem builds its unique, expressive structure of likeness and unlikeness. The couplet scheme (conventionally notated as *aabb*) of end-rhyme in "The dry soul rages"; the alternating scheme (conventionally notated as *abab*) of end-rhyme in "The Darkling Thrush" or "To Earth-ward"; the elaborate *abbbacccbb* that swirls through the first stanza of "My Picture Left in Scotland"; the absence of end-rhyme in "An Old Man's Winter Night" or "The Snow Man" or "Howl"—these paradigms tell only a little about the chiming and echoing of vowel and consonant in the actual works.

As with other aspects of the sound of a poem, rhymed and unrhymed are not only matters of degree, infinitely varied; they also vary, expressively, in the context of all the other aspects of the poem. Hearing as much of that variation as possible is the goal.

BLANK VERSE AND

FREE VERSE

I have suggested a series of analogies between elements of sound, based on the way pairs of elements vary significantly in relation to each other. The play between pitch and duration, between syntax and line, between like and unlike sounds, becomes a means of art. These are comparable ways to achieve meaning and feeling.

In this final chapter I want to propose a similar, but more conceptual, play between the rhythms in a free-verse poem and the recalled experience—by reader and writer—of the rhythms in iambic poems, of which I will take blank verse as a great, representative type. This duality, too—the play between free-verse rhythms and iambic rhythms—can be an artistic means toward meaning and feeling.

To hear free verse, and to write it effectively, is a demanding skill. In that sense, all true poetry is "formal": the form in some cases is based on a measure, in others it is not. I think that an understanding of blank verse in particular, among the iambic measures, can help one hear more accurately and elegantly the rhythms of free verse. This final chapter will consist largely of some examples of that principle, which I will try to draw from some contemporary poems written in extremely effective free verse.

Blank verse (unrhymed lines based on a norm of five iambic feet) has had a predominant role in poetry written in English. This predominance, historically, has been considerable. Free verse might be described as the most successful alternative to pentameters. Ezra Pound, speaking of formal developments early in the twentieth century, wrote in a much quoted formulation: "to break the pentameter, that was the first heave."

Writing in 1918, Pound noted the widening adaptation and—in his view—dilution of free verse; he complains:

Indeed *vers libre* has become as prolix and verbose as any of the flaccid varieties that preceded it. It has brought faults of its own. The actual language and phrasing is often as bad as that of our elders without even the excuse that the words are shoveled in to fill a metric pattern or to complete the noise of a rhyme-sound. Whether or no the phrases followed by the followers are musical must be left to the reader's decision. At times I can find a marked meter in "vers libres," as stale and hackneyed as any pseudo-Swinburnian, at times the writers seem to follow no musical structure whatever.[1]

The standard this passage brings to free verse is like the standard that inspired the free-verse movement early in the century: a standard of freshness, expressiveness and musicality. Blank verse, in its oppressive staleness, in its evergreen possibilities, in its monumental history, and in its tendency to underlie writing of other kinds—free, measured, even in prose—provides an important basis for comprehension.

To show what I mean, I will return to one of the first examples in this book, Frost's "To Earthward." My purpose is to move from this poem to the pentameter measure and from there to free verse. As we've seen, the poem is in lines of three and two feet ("trimeter" and "dimeter"): three trimeters in each stanza, followed by one dimeter:

Love at the lips was touch
As sweet as I could bear;
And once that seemed too much;
I lived on air

That crossed me from sweet things,
The flow of—was it musk
From hidden grapevine springs
Downhill at dusk?

Notice that because the poem is written in threes and twos, it contains fives; that is, contained in the structure are pentameters, the five feet of:

And once that seemed too much; I lived on air

And also, overlapping that hidden, but audible, line, an-
other pentameter, the five feet of:

I lived on air that crossed me from sweet things

There are "buried" or contained pentameters within the
poem, some of them beginning or ending at the caesura.
This observation suggests that measures and rhythms
may sometimes overlap and coincide and diverge again.

The three-plus-two line, the line concealed in the
stanzaic form of "To Earthward," has been one of the
main sorts of blank-verse line. Sometimes the pause
moves to near the end, and the line appears as a four-
plus-one:

But if the while I think on thee, dear friend

Or with the pause earlier, as a one-plus-four:

Second, the conscious impotence of rage[2]

Or as any of many other variations that divide five feet
with a pause.

It is worth noting that the four-and-one division
means that the pentameter line also contains a four-foot
or tetrameter rhythm: varying the two-and-three divi-
sion of the "To Earthward" stanza or of five-foot lines
divided into two and three feet. This capacity to contain
other measures, or to flicker into them at times, is an-

other aspect of the pentameter line, much exploited by Shakespeare in the plays.

The pause may come in the middle of a foot; and with the variations in pitch, duration, and how the syntax falls in relation to line ending and pause, the number of variations approaches infinity. And yet this same, five-foot frame for fixed-and-variable treatment can seem obnoxiously formulaic. The degree of appeal and tedium in pentameters varies considerably, depending at least in part upon the mood and predilections of the reader, as well as the talent of the writer.

Both the potential attraction and the potential monotony of this line have proved remarkable, on the historical record. The pentameter line can become eloquence itself, and it can sink into trite formulas. Pound's description of getting away from the pentameter as "the first heave" of his modernist enterprise has repeated itself more than once, for other writers since the beginning of the modern period.

For example, many poets of the generation of Americans born in the late nineteen-twenties began their careers writing pentameters and abandoned them. To name just a few, Robert Bly, Galway Kinnell, Philip Levine, Adrienne Rich, and James Wright all published first books with pentameter poems, ranging from adequate but wooden in rhythm to quite beautiful. My personal observation is that those who wrote the best, most striking pentameters went on to write the most attractive free verse. Here, for example, is a passage from an early poem by James Wright, "A Presentation of Two Birds to My Son"; the writing seems to me extremely beautiful, though in some ways the sensibility that comes up with the phrases "he hardly flies on brains" and "pockets of air impale his hollow bones" seems somewhat caged or restless within the way the pentameter lines are handled:

Look up and see the swift above the trees.
How shall I tell you why he always veers
And banks away from the shaken sleeve of air,
Away from ground? He hardly flies on brains;
Pockets of air impale his hollow bones.
He leans against the rainfall or the sun.

One could meld this passage onto a continuous stream of blank verse, concealing the join between passages from Shakespeare and Milton, then continuing the sentences from, say, a descriptive passage in *Paradise Lost* into Wordsworth, and from Wordsworth into the Stevens of "Sunday Morning" and then Frost or the Eliot of "Four Quartets," and perhaps contrive a slide through Roethke into this passage from Wright's poem, and then into some of the pentameters I have winkled out of Ginsberg's "Howl."

Observing how Wright's pentameter lines are put together largely in units of two feet (e.g., "pockets of air," "Look up and see," "away from ground") and three feet (e.g., "the swift above the trees," "the shaken sleeve of air," "he hardly flies on brains"), sometimes overlapping, the reader might recall the threes and twos of "To Earthward." But at least one of the lines, the first, might be divided by the caesura into one foot and four: "Look up," we might hear, "and see the swift above the trees."

Hearing those units of two, three, and four feet, and hearing the iambs, light or heavy or in between, in some counterpoint or resistance to the idiosyncratic utterance, is good preparation, I think, for hearing lines that often can't quite be divided into feet, and clusters of syllables that pull away from the iambic pattern—as in a late, free-verse poem by Wright, "The First Days" (the epigraph is *"Optima dies fugit"*):

> The first thing I saw in the morning
> Was a huge golden bee ploughing
> His burly right shoulder into the belly
> Of a sleek yellow pear
> Low on a bough.
> Before he could find that sudden black honey
> That squirms around in there
> Inside the seed, the tree could not bear any more.
> The pear fell to the ground,
> With the bee still half alive
> Inside its body.

The first two lines alternate clusters of relatively stressed syllables packed together—like the four syllables "first thing I saw," and the spondaic-sounding "huge gold" and "bee plough"—with clusters of relatively light syllables, like the last syllable of "morning" and the first two syllables of the next line. Yet "Was a huge golden bee," isolated by itself, could be one of the threes in "To Earthward," or part of a pentameter. The movement of the opening lines, in other words, mediates between a kind of allusion or echo of iambic verse and a refusal of that movement. Similarly, the line "Before he could find that sudden black honey" teases toward a pentameter and declines to be one, while "Low on a bough" and "That squirms around in there," on either side of the longer line, are units of two and three feet—or would be in a poem that maintained an iambic norm.

To hear these lines avoiding pentameter is to hear more about them.

I don't mean to imply that one must know pentameter to know poetry, or to hear it. On the contrary, it is clear that great poetry has been written by poets who wrote little or no iambic pentameter—though they must have heard a lot of it, I think: whether in Yeats, Eliot, Stevens, Wordsworth, Milton, Donne, or Shakespeare.

Neither do I mean to say that Wright "had to" abandon iambs or pentameter—he never entirely did, in fact—in order to compose his poems authentically. It has been claimed that pentameter is not a contemporary, or not an American, measure. Possibly this is true only until the next great poet makes it no longer true. It has been claimed that people, or Americans in particular, do not speak in iambic pentameter. But sometimes we do. Consider these examples:

All politics is local politics.

Excuse me: can you tell me how to get
To Monmouth Park, in Oceanport, from here?

Well come on, Baby, take a whiff on me.

Or, in the Shakespearean style of dividing pentameters among speakers:

> *C.:* Look—when the guy that plays first base picks up
>   His check, his *name* is written on it, right?
> *A.:* Of course it is!
> *C.:*   Whose name?
> *A.:*   That's right.
> *C.:*   What's right?
> *A.:* No, what's the name of the guy on second base!
> *C.:* Ah, bocka-docka, bucka docka *baah!*

Often, there does not seem much more than a theoretical point in recalling pentameter, or the iambic forms to which pentameter is central. In some of the contemporary free verse I admire, there is far less presence of the pentameter, or of the threes and twos, than in the "Who's on First?" routine. For example, here are the opening four lines of C. K. Williams's poem "Tar."

The long, end-stopped lines would not be mistaken for pentameter, or any other iambic measure:

> The first morning of Three Mile Island: those first
> > disquieting, uncertain, mystifying hours.
> All morning a crew of workmen have been tearing
> > the old decrepit roof off our building,
> and all morning, trying to distract myself, I've been
> > wandering out to watch them
> as they hack away the leaden layers of asbestos
> > paper and disassemble the disintegrating
> > drains.

Common sense suggests that long lines are more likely to be end-stopped while shorter lines are more likely to involve enjambment. But there is a phenomenon within these long lines that is like the enjambments of Ben Jonson's "My Picture Left in Scotland." In that poem, lines of various length make a graceful set of platforms—of five feet, or four, or three, or two, or one —for the sentence to dance across, Astaire-like:

> I now think, Love is rather deaf than blind,
> > For else it could not be
> > > That she
> Whom I adore so much should so slight me,
> > And cast my love behind.
> I'm sure my language to her was as sweet,
> > And every close did meet

> In sentence of as subtle feet
> As hath the youngest he
> That sits in shadow of Apollo's tree.

The syntactical energy continuing through rhythmic units of various length is part of the charm and force of this stanza. And so, too, the pauses inside the long free-verse lines of "Tar" mark off, without halting, parts of a syntactical energy, as can be indicated by imposing a different typography:

> The first morning of Three Mile Island:
> those first disquieting,
> uncertain,
> mystifying hours.

This hesitant series of short units is followed by something very close to a pentameter (anapest in the second position):

> All morning a crew of workmen have been tearing
> the old decrepit roof off our building,

And there is something like the Ben Jonson poem, too, in the way C. K. Williams ends his sentence with a long, resolving unit; again, I'll tamper with his lines to make a point, and arrange them so they end with a line of blank verse (though it requires a run-over in the middle of a word):

and all morning,
trying to distract myself,
I've been wandering out to watch them
as they hack away
the leaden layers of asbestos paper and dis-
assemble the disintegrating drains.

The rhythm of pauses, the alternation of longer and shorter units, the flirting with iambic rhythms (as in the second "line" above, which is close to trimeter, or the buried pentameter "line" made by "the leaden layers of asbestos paper"): all of these are expressive, tracing among other things a contrast between the tentative definition of the psychological state in the poem's opening line and the confident demolition described in the longer units. The repeated phrase "All morning" takes two different cadences in a way that recalls the expressively partial or varied parallelisms of Frost's "An Old Man's Winter Night."

It probably is a good idea to restore the opening of "Tar" to its proper typography; the lines are neither short nor iambic. In fact, the keeping together of rather stressed syllables (as in the first three syllables of "Three Mile Island" or the first two syllables of "all morning" and of "uncertain") muffles the iambic potential, brings out a far different movement. And though the typography is notation for what we hear, the long lines do tell us that the pauses marking off elements of different

lengths are part of a larger cadence or symmetry, the
long units of roughly equal length:

> The first morning of Three Mile Island: those first
> disquieting, uncertain, mystifying hours.
> All morning a crew of workmen have been tearing
> the old decrepit roof off our building,
> and all morning, trying to distract myself, I've been
> wandering out to watch them
> as they hack away the leaden layers of asbestos
> paper and disassemble the disintegrating
> drains.

The art of the poem is that it achieves an intense ca
dence that is neither prose nor iambic: that is one way
of defining "free verse."

(The arbitrary, typographical breaks required by the
fact that Williams's lines are longer than this page is
wide should be instructive. The typesetter's (or page-
maker's) breaks, determined by the physical dimensions
of the page, are conventionally or functionally invisible
in relation to the sound. The line is vocal, a sound; the
typographical arrangement is a notation for that sound.)

The pause that separates units of varying length is a
powerful aspect of the gorgeous sixteenth-century poems
that inspire the rhythms of Frost and Stevens, like these
lines of Thomas Campion's, a series of unexpected sym-

metries and asymmetries that explode into the longer unit in the fourth line:

Follow your saint, follow with accents sweet,
Haste you, sad notes, fall at her flying feet:
There, wrapped in cloud of sorrow, pity move,
And tell the ravisher of my soul I perish for her
love.

Just as rhythms like Campion's clearly underlie "To Earthward," in free-verse poems, too, we can find kinds of movement related to Campion's starts and stops, from the relatively standard two-three division of his first line to the non-standard pauses in the third line—midway in the first foot, and before the three syllables "pity move."

Listen, for example, to the way short units of varying lengths give life and force to the grammatical parallelisms of this passage in Louise Glück's "Mock Orange":

It is not the moon, I tell you.
It is these flowers
lighting the yard.

I hate them.
I hate them as I hate sex,
the man's mouth
sealing my mouth, the man's
paralyzing body—

and the cry that always escapes,
the low, humiliating
premise of union—

In my mind tonight
I hear the question and pursuing answer
fused in one sound
that mounts and mounts and then
is split into the old selves,
the tired antagonisms. Do you see?
We were made tools of.
And the scent of mock orange
drifts through the window.

Glück's parallel phrases ("It is not . . . It is . . ." or "I hate . . . I hate"), as in the example by Campion ("Follow . . . follow"), put the repeated word into units of different length, with an effect of movement or dynamism coursing through the stasis of repetition. Her "I hate them," shorter than the units before and after, has an effect something like that of "There," and "pity move" in Campion's lines. And as Campion releases the energy built up by the pauses into the hypertrophied long fourth line, with relatively little caesura, Glück's enjambment of a long grammatical unit creates an aesthetic and emotional release:

In my mind tonight
I hear the question and pursuing answer

fused in one sound
that mounts and mounts and then
is split into the old selves,
the tired antagonisms. Do you see?

And as that movement, the grammar swelling across the line, subsides, the short unit "Do you see?" echoes the earlier "I hate them." But in effect, in another sense, "Do you see" also echoes "pity move."

Shakespeare made pentameter lines out of single words or phrases such as "never" or "and to-morrow"; so, too, in a free-verse poem, does Frank Bidart. What is interesting is how the blank-verse rhythm overlaps rhythms that are not iambic at all, surging into the poem and then out of it. Here is all of the poem, Bidart's "Overheard Through the Walls of the Invisible City":

. . . telling those who swarm around him his desire
is that an appendage from each of them
fill, invade each of his orifices,—

repeating, chanting,
Oh yeah   O yeah   O yeah   O yeah   Oh yeah

until, as if in darkness he craved the sun, at last he
   reached
consummation.

> —Until telling those who swarm around him
> begins again

> (we are the wheel to which we are bound).

The line of *"Oh yeah"* five times is a pentameter, but so too is the first part of the next line,

> until, as if in darkness he craved the sun,

with an anapest in the fourth position. Another overlapping pentameter is

> as if in darkness he craved the sun, at last

Thus, the phrases "until" and "at last"—each of them excluded from one of these overlapping pentameters—the more prominently echo the one-iamb unit of *"Oh yeah."* I think that, without thinking about it or naming the phenomenon, we hear such cadences, and the presence of the older rhythms moving through such passages and out of them. This kind of hearing is what makes free verse have the intensity of verse.

My final example, the final poem quoted in this book, is from James McMichael's "Itinerary," a narrative poem that goes from West to East, and backward in time, from a contemporary setting in the Western mountains to the East Coast and Colonial Virginia. Various American diarists are quoted or alluded to along the way. The be-

ginning of the poem is in an eloquent, highly cadenced
free verse:

> The farmhouses north of Driggs,
> silos for miles along the road saying
> BUTLER or SIOUX. The light saying
> rain coming on, the wind not up yet,
> animals waiting as the front hits
> everything on the high flats, hailstones
> bouncing like rabbits under the sage.

This free-verse description segues gradually through the
adventures of Lewis and Clark and others, the cadences
varying as the idiom does. Here is the poem's conclusion,
in which McMichael, one of the most innovative and
experimental of contemporary poets, allows his poem to
break, gradually, into blank verse:

> This walk is news. Its bodies point me always
> in and out along some newer course.
> There have been divers days together
> wherein alone I've watched these flowers
> buoyed on their stems and holding up the sun.
> Just now I catch them thinking on themselves,
> composing from their dark places the least
> passages for light, tendering how they look
> and how I look on them. It comes to me
> that the world is to the end of it
> thinking on itself and how its parts

gather with one another for their time.
These are the light, and all the forms they show
are lords of inns wherein the soul takes rest.
If I could find it in myself to hide
the world within the world then there would be
no place to which I could remove it; save
that brightness wherein all things come to see.

It is with the seventh line from the end, "gather with one another for their time," that the blank verse fully takes over. But the whole passage trembles toward that cadence (and in the line "Just now I catch them thinking on themselves" shudders right into it). The structure of McMichael's poem, a journey through landscape into the past, seems to have required this unexpected formal arrival.

I invite the reader to read this passage aloud, and to take pleasure in the sounds of it. Though the lines are about a kind of ecstatic perception, in context of the poem which journeys back in history they are also about memory. Most writers who consider the subject of poetry's origins associate the art of verse with memory: the griots in Alex Haley's *Roots* preserve detailed information, reaching back many generations, without written records, by using a technology of recurrent sounds. Rhymes and emphatic rhythms help us to memorize. Verse in this way is a technology for memory, using the sounds of language, created by a human body, as writing uses marks.

Blank verse is perhaps less easily memorized than end-rhymed verse, and free verse is perhaps less easily memorized than blank verse. Nevertheless, poetry's cadences and its patterns of like sounds persist in all these forms, embodying the deep, ancient links that join memory, human intelligence, culture, and the sounds of spoken language. In the particular physical presence of memorable language we can find a reminder of our ability to know and retain knowledge itself: the "brightness wherein all things come to see."

I have tried to show ways to hear more of what poems accomplish, and thereby to take more pleasure in them. What I have tried to heighten in the reader is not the ability to write or speak about technical aspects of poetry but the ability to read poetry with insight into the vocal nature of the art.

The test of success is not in reproducing my vocabulary, but in the experience of reading.

Implicitly, I have been addressing poets, in particular young poets, as well as readers. To both groups, my advice for further study is to identify a poem one loves, to read it aloud, perhaps to write it longhand or type it out, and to get at least some of it by heart. Having done that, do the same with another poem, and with many more. I offer this advice not as a sentimental parting salute but as a stringent invitation to study. For an art is best understood through careful attention to great examples.

As Yeats says in the lines I have taken for my epigraph:

Nor is there singing school, but studying
Monuments of its own magnificence.

Notes

Introduction

1. Frost uses this phrase, and enlarges on it, in a letter of July 4, 1913, to John T. Bartlett (*Frost, Collected Poems, Prose and Plays*, ed. Richard Poirier, p. 664–69). On this subject I also recommend Frost's great essay "The Figure a Poem Makes," a brief prose piece which Frost included in every collected poems published during his lifetime. The essay is unaccountably omitted from the defective *Collected Poems* edited by Edward Connery Lathem, but included in the Poirier volume (published by the Library of America).

2. The quotations are from poems by, in the order quoted, William Butler Yeats ("The Folly of Being Comforted"), Elizabeth Bishop ("Over 1,000 Illustrations and a Complete Concordance"), Fulke Greville (*Caelica* #69, "When all this All doth pass from age to age"), Robert Frost ("Directive"), Wallace Stevens ("The Emperor of Ice Cream"), Emily Dickinson (#1068), and William Carlos Williams ("The Widow's Lament in Springtime").

I / ACCENT AND DURATION

1. Ben Jonson, "To the Immortal Memory and Friendship of That Noble Pair, Sir Lucius Carey and Sir Henry Morrison."
2. Thomas Campion, "Now Winter Nights Enlarge."

1. *Ben Jonson: The Complete Poems*, ed. George Parfitt, New Haven 1975. I have taken the liberty of modernizing punctuation, partly in order to make my point here.

2. "First position" examples: William Shakespeare, *Richard III*; Wallace Stevens, "Sunday Morning"; Emily Dickinson, #1068; Shakespeare, Sonnet 30; Robert Browning, "My Last Duchess"; John Keats, "On First Looking into Chapman's Homer"; Robert Frost, "Mending Wall."

   "Second position" examples: John Keats, "Ode to a Nightingale"; Thomas Nashe, "Litany in Time of Plague"; Yvor Winters, "A Summer Commentary"; Robert Frost, "To Earthward."

   "Third position" examples: Shakespeare, Sonnet 30; John Milton, "Lycidas"; Philip Larkin, "Church Going."

   "Fourth position" examples: Louise Bogan, "Song for the Last Act"; William Butler Yeats, "Leda and the Swan."

3. William Wordsworth, The Prelude, Book I, line 340.

4. Robert Frost, "To Earthward."

5. William Carlos Williams, "To a Poor Old Woman."

III / TECHNICAL TERMS AND VOCAL REALITIES

1. Lines from the following previously discussed poems: "To Earthward" (Frost); "Now Winter Nights Enlarge" (Campion); "My Picture Left in Scotland" (Jonson).

2. William Shakespeare (Sonnet 30); Robert Frost ("In a Poem"); Wallace Stevens ("The House Was Quiet and the World Was Calm"); Elizabeth Bishop ("Over 1,000 Illustrations and a Complete Concordance"); Thomas Campion ("When Thou Must Home to Shades of Underground").

3. William Shakespeare, Sonnet 30.

4. John Thompson, in *The Founding of English Meter*, offers a brilliant,

lucid theory: that the iamb is the most elegant, because the simplest, model of two predominant characteristics of spoken English: its accentual character, and the tendency of the strongest accent in a sequence of accents to find its way as nearly as possible to the end of the appropriate grammatical-syntactical unit (phrase, clause, sentence).

5. W. S. Gilbert, "When You're Lying Awake with a Dismal Headache" (the Lord Chancellor's song from *Iolanthe*).

6. Fulke Greville, *Caelica*, #56.

IV / LIKE AND UNLIKE SOUNDS

1. J. V. Cunningham, "Epigram 16."

V / BLANK VERSE AND FREE VERSE

1. *Literary Essays of Ezra Pound*, p. 3.

2. T. S. Eliot, "Little Gidding."

Index of Names and Terms

NOTE · I have included in **bold face** a few terms that are not used in the main text of this book but that readers may encounter elsewhere and want defined. My definitions are cursory, particularly in relation to "received forms" like **sestina** and **villanelle**, which I confess do not much interest me. For more complete definitions, and more terms, an excellent reference work is *The Princeton Encyclopedia of Poetry and Poetics*. See also the works I mention in the Introduction.

accentual meter. A structural principle wherein the lines of a poem have a certain number of accents, while the position and degree of accent varies, as does the number of syllables. This meter has never been much used in English, perhaps because the varying degree of accent makes such lines hard to hear. The iambic, **accentual-syllabic** line has predominated, maybe because determining the accent within the foot is more intuitive or feasible. Here is an example of three-accent lines, from Edgar Bowers's poem "Dark Earth and Summer":

Earth is dark where you rest
Though a little winter grass
Glistens in icy furrows.
There, cautious as I pass,

Squirrels run, leaving stains
Of their nervous, minute feet
Over the tombs; and near them
Birds gray and gravely sweet.

This sounds good to me, but more in the way of a good free-verse poem than in the way of a poem in iambs.

accentual-syllabic meter. A structural principle wherein the lines of a poem have a certain number of feet. This term refers to the kind of meter, based on the iambic foot, which has historically predominated in English verse. It is called "accentual-syllabic" because the foot is defined both by its syllables and by the placement of an accent within it. I more often use the term "iambic lines" or "iambic meter" because that is nearly always what it is, and the phrase seems to me to give more useful information.

alliteration. The recurrence of like consonant sounds at the beginnings of words or syllables, as in "through the threatening throng."

assonance. A repeated vowel sound, as in "bake" and "claim."

caesura. The pause or break within a line, as after the first three words in "She fears him, and will always ask."

consonance. A repeated consonant sound, as in "stroke" and "ache."

couplet. Two successive, rhyming lines. More loosely, two lines set off typographically.

monosyllabic foot, 65

Nashe, Thomas, 32, 67–68

O'Hara, Frank, 92

pitch, 15, 56, 65, 81, 97, 101

Plath, Sylvia, 58, 70

poetry. I will be content in this book to accept a social, cultural defi-
nition of poetry: poetry is what a bookstore puts in the section of that
name. From such a definition one can proceed to discuss the kind of
poetry one prefers or admires, etc.

Pound, Ezra, 8, 98–99, 101

prose poem. A poem written in prose rather than lines.

pyrrhic foot, 65

quatrain. A **stanza** of four lines.

rhyme. The sound of words with like endings. See Chapter III.

rhythm and meter, 51–59

Rich, Adrienne, 101

Robinson, Edwin Arlington, 76

Roethke, Theodore, 67

sestet. A **stanza** or unit of six lines, particularly the last six lines of a
sonnet.

sestina. A set or "received" form for a poem of six six-line stanzas plus
a final three-line stanza, involving the recurrence of a selected six
words at the ends of lines in each of the first six stanzas, in a certain
sequence; the words are also repeated, two in each line, in the final
stanza. An excellent definition can be deduced from reading Elizabeth
Bishop's poem "Sestina."

Shakespeare, William, 31, 52, 56, 58–59, 61, 67, 71, 73, 101, 102, 104,
112

Sidney, Philip, 58, 75

sonnet. (From the Italian for "little song.") A poem written within a
set form of fourteen lines, normally of iambic pentameter, frequently
rhymed as three alternately rhymed **quatrains** followed by a **couplet**
or as two alternately rhymed or *abba* quatrains followed by six lines

rhymed in the pattern *abcabc*. In the traditional sonnet, modeled on Philip Sidney's sequence *Astrophel and Stella*, the rhyme scheme corresponds to turns in the argument, the poem is part of a loosely plotted sequence, and the theme is extravagant sexual courtship or seduction. From a form based on the rhetorical display of courtship, the sonnet evolved over decades and centuries to accommodate many kinds of feeling and subject matter. Immensely popular in the 1590s, the sonnet became a kind of playing field for poetic rhetoric, ingenuity, emulation, and experiment.

stanza. A division of a poem, set off typographically by white space above and below it. Strictly speaking, a stanza has a set, recurring number of lines in a pattern; loosely speaking, the term is used to refer to any verse paragraph.

syllabic meter. A structural principle wherein the lines of a poem contain a certain number of syllables, while the placement of accents and quantities varies. This meter has never been much used in English, perhaps because the variations in accent and duration make it extremely hard—virtually impossible—to hear how many syllables there are in a line. Possibly the most celebrated and excellent poet to count syllables in English to make her lines is Marianne Moore. I hear her lines as excellent free verse; the syllable count seems more or less arbitrary to me.

Here are the first two stanzas of Moore's rhymed, syllabic poem "The Fish":

The Fish

wade
through black-jade.

Of the crow-blue mussel-shells, one keeps
adjusting the ash heaps;
opening and closing itself like

an
injured fan.
The barnacles which encrust the side
of the wave cannot hide
there for the submerged shafts of the

This sounds very good to me, but while my fingers tell me that there
are nine syllables in each stanza's third line, my ear cannot.

syllable. Surprisingly hard to define. Rather than try, I will acknowledge
that fact here, in the hopes that conceding the slipperiness of this
seemingly straightforward notion may encourage those readers who
have trouble hearing the word "syllable" itself as a three-syllable
word, or the word "trailed" as only one syllable. There is a story
about a writing student from Alabama who asked his teacher how
many syllables are in the word "fire." Informed that the answer is
"one," the student responded that, in the South, it contains four.

tercet. A **stanza** of three lines.

villanelle. A set form for a poem of nineteen lines: five three-line stanzas
and a concluding four-line stanza, using only two rhymes throughout.
The first and third lines of the initial stanza, which rhyme, take turns
recurring as a concluding, refrain line in the next four stanzas. Then,
in the final, four-line stanza, the two refrain lines become the final
two lines of the poem, so that the two refrains recur one after the
other as a conclusion. The second lines of all five three-line stanzas
rhyme. An excellent definition can be deduced from reading Dylan
Thomas's poem "Do Not Go Gentle into That Good Night."

Although great poems have been written in received forms, the
complex scaffolding often leads the writer to substitute patience and

ingenuity for actual formal accomplishment. To write "in a form" is not necessarily to write with form, a quality that appears in the free-verse poems of Williams and Stevens. As to "forms," I believe that George Herbert invented an interesting one nearly every time he wrote a poem.